EXPLOSIVE RUNNING

EXPLOSIVE RUNNING

Using the Science of Kinesiology to Improve Your Performance

Michael Yessis, Ph.D.

McGraw Hill

New York   Chicago   San Francisco   Lisbon   London   Madrid   Mexico City
Milan   New Delhi   San Juan   Seoul   Singapore   Sydney   Toronto

Library of Congress Cataloging-in-Publication Data

Yessis, Michael.
    Explosive running : using the science of kinesiology to improve your performance /
Michael Yessis.
        p. cm.
    Includes index.
    ISBN 0-8092-9899-6
    1. Running—Physiological aspects.   2. Kinesiology.   I. Title.

RC1220.R8 Y47   2000
613.7'172—dc21   99-59335

6 7 8 9 10 11 12 13 14 15 16 17 18 19 20 21 22   VLP/VLP   0 9 8 7 6

ISBN-13: 978-0-8092-9899-0
ISBN-10:   0-8092-9899-6

Cover design by Nick Panos
Cover photograph copyright © Mike Powell/Allsport
Interior design by Precision Graphics
Interior photographs by Michael Yessis

Please note that the quality of the images reproduced in this book is because a digital
video camera was used to capture the action of running. The author and publisher
believe that this method is best suited to the purpose and intention of the book. The
digital camera captures motion better than any other photographic medium easily
available today, though the images do not reproduce as well as conventional images.

This book is dedicated to aspiring runners. I hope it gives you the ability to run well so that you can get all the enjoyment possible from this great sport.

Contents

Acknowledgments

I am deeply indebted to many people who have helped make this book possible. Without their assistance and sometimes perseverance, this book would not have its many unique and informative features. The order in which the names appear is not related to the importance of the work and the assistance they provided. More specifically, I would like to thank:

- Glen Reyes, one of the models who is a sprinter featured in this book. His early running improvement allowed him to win the 100- and 200-yard events in the San Diego High School championships, and he continues to perform well today. He now assists in teaching the Yessis method.
- Jeff Berman, a high school runner specializing in the 200-yard run, who also runs the 100 and 400 as needed, and who served as a model for the running and the exercise pictures. His increases in speed have been truly amazing.
- Jose Barbosa, 800 and 1,500 meters, is a four-time Olympian (best was fourth place) and who was also a gold, silver, and bronze medal winner in six world championships. He is now working toward his fifth Olympic appearance and is one of the models.

- John Campbell, outstanding track sprinter and running back in football. One of the models for the running and the exercise photographs.
- Edgar Oliveira, Olympian who participated in Barcelona and Atlanta in the 1,500 meters.
- Joaó N'tiamba, who participated in three Olympic games in the 800 and 1,500 meters but who now runs the 5,000 and 10,000 meters.
- Wander Moura, a model who runs the 3,000 steeplechase. He holds the South American record and has participated in the Olympics and World Championships. He won in the last Pan-American games.
- Steve Metz, one of the models who was a good sprinter in track (10.6 seconds in the 100 meter and 22.5 seconds in the 200 meter) and who was an outstanding wide receiver in football.
- Dr. Jerry Moyland, a chiropractor and marathoner in the San Diego area who was very helpful in contacting some of the models.
- Terri Moyland, who has run almost all the major marathons from Boston to Hawaii, who served as a model.
- Sherrill Brady, a former pro-triathlete whose best marathon time is 2:56, for serving as a model.

- Paul Thomas, a professional dual athlete and 1999 national champion, for being one of the models.
- Jacob Young, one of the models for the exercises, who is also a runner and good all-around athlete.
- Chad Young, high school runner, specializing mainly in the 800-yard dash, who served as one of the models for the exercises.
- David Dominguez, top marathon runner in the San Diego area, who served as a model for marathon running technique.
- Jason M. Lewis, marathoner, one of the models for long-distance running technique.
- Brian Culley, a model for running technique, who is one of the top marathon runners in the San Diego area, who is now getting ready to try out for the U.S. Olympic team.
- Josh Cox, one of the top marathon runners in the San Diego area and one of the models for running technique.
- Dr. Tobin Watkinson, a renowned clinical nutritionist and good friend, for his invaluable assistance in preparing the chapter on nutrition.
- Marissa Yessis, my daughter, who labored long and hard importing and preparing each individual frame and picture used in the book.
- Edie Yessis, my loving wife, who had put up with me during the hectic days of getting the manuscript and pictures together.
- Ken Samelson, my acquisitions editor, NTC/Contemporary Publishing Group, who was very helpful in the initial stages of preparing this book and in the early edits.
- Nancy Hall, project editor, NTC/Contemporary Publishing Group, who worked closely with me in finalizing the book.
- Greg McMillan, editor of *Peak Running Performance,* for his assistance in contacting runners to serve as models.

Introduction

Running is easy; everyone can do it. All you have to do is put one leg in front of the other faster than you do in walking. Since everyone can run, it is commonly believed that running must be a natural activity, and everyone is born with this ability—you only have to run more to become better or faster. If you believe this, you will never achieve your best in running or in any other sport that requires running.

If you are a serious student of running you will want to improve your ability so you can consistently run better for greater speed and distance without injury. It can be done! You only need to perfect your running technique and develop your physical abilities as they relate to running. When you can duplicate the same basic running pattern on every stride in every run for maximum speed, distance, and efficiency, you will have achieved your genetic potential.

Accomplishing this goal is not especially hard. If you listen to conventional wisdom, you will get better shoes, more professional coaching, and do more running. Many runners have tried these routes and spent hours on the track (or road) trying to improve only to end up frustrated or injured. There are, however, more simple ways to perfect your running. Regardless of the equipment you use or the recommendations given to you by a coach, you must have the physical ability to run well, and as far and fast as you desire. You must have the strength and flexibility to execute the needed joint actions. If you do not, you are doomed to failure regardless how much money you spend, how many lessons you take, and how much practice you put in. *Your run will only be as good as your physical abilities allow.*

Making a few simple changes to improve your strength, flexibility, speed of movement, and technique will improve your running beyond your wildest expectations. This book will show you how, using a method I have developed after working with thousands of runners. The concepts of improving technique and your physical ability cannot be overemphasized. As brought out previously, this is the basis of the Yessis method that, after being used with thousands of runners, has proven its value many times over. In essence, in order to improve your running, you must improve technique, improve your physical abilities as they relate to your technique, and perfect these two factors as they are coupled together in the total running action. Only then can you truly improve speed to its maximum. I have seen these runners significantly improve their speed and distance by merely making changes in their technique and improving their physical abilities specific to running.

In addition, by modifying technique or doing special strength and flexibility exercises, runners who had typically experienced problems such as back or leg pain during or after running found their pain soon disappeared. Still others found it easier to maintain body balance and rhythm during the run because of stronger support muscles and greater control and feel for muscle actions. Without exception, all runners experienced improvement in their running after undertaking individualized programs to improve technique by doing special exercises specific to their run. When physical training to increase strength and flexibility is coupled with speed training the results are even more impressive.

Reading *Explosive Running* may be the first step on your pathway to getting the fullest possible enjoyment and satisfaction from running. If you carry out the recommendations in this book you will be amazed at how much progress you can make in a relatively short time. This applies not only to simply making changes in your running technique, but also to any particular physical problems you may have. For example, many runners are plagued by lower-back problems. But lower-back problems are some of the easiest to take care of! Although this may sound hard to believe, it has been proved time and time again with runners and with athletes in other sports as well. In this book you will see how you, too, can run pain-free.

Although the book contains a great deal of information, I have made a serious attempt to present it in a simple and straightforward manner. Also included are actual sequence pictures of runners and exercises that are specific to the key actions in the running stride. Thus you should not think of this book as merely a book on special exercises for running; approach it as something that will give you a better understanding of running and how you can improve your running in the shortest amount of time.

You are on the starting line. Do you wish to attack the run and do better than ever, or would you rather continue to run the same old way and achieve the same old results? Your success or failure is up to you! If you follow the recommendations given in this book, I guarantee you will see outstanding results.

EXPLOSIVE RUNNING

Improve Your Run Dramatically

The many books and articles on running attest not only to the popularity of running, but also to its individuality. One can see just about as many different running styles as there are different running tracks and courses. The individuality of running leads to confusion as to what constitutes effective running technique, how to prevent injury, and how to increase speed or distance.

There are also disagreements regarding key running actions. For example, a runner came to me who had been to more than ten different running coaches seeking a better understanding of his running. According to him, each one told him something different about his running, making him even more confused.

Regardless of your running technique, there are specific key actions everyone must execute in order to have a successful run. How well you execute these actions depends on your physical capabilities. More specifically, your physical abilities determine: (1) how much you rely on each joint action, (2) the range of motion of each action, and (3) the force involved in each action in the running stride.

It is not uncommon to read a description of what occurs in running, but an analysis—especially a bio-mechanical analysis—is quite different. An analysis answers questions such as: If the run is effective, why is it effective? What is the role of each joint action? Which actions can be changed to make the technique more effective? How can the specific actions be made more powerful? Should the running technique be modified, and if so, how? Most standard instruction does not address these points.

Rarely is there agreement among coaches and teachers as to why a particular action is needed, why a particular action must occur, why it should precede another action, why a certain action is most effective, how it is best executed, the best sequence of actions needed to produce maximum speed or economy, or how each action makes its contribution to prepare for the next action or phase of running. Instead, we see articles related to the opinions of runners and coaches (and in many cases, shoe companies), which are often at odds with one another.

I am confident you have seen articles dealing with whether the heel, ball of the foot, or whole foot makes first contact on touchdown. From biomechanics we know that the heel hit can cause injury and that it slows you down because of the braking forces produced. These forces (generated when the heel hits the ground), which momentarily stop lower-body movement, can be extremely high and are usually the culprit in many leg and foot injuries. Equally important is that the heel hit does not utilize the economical and speed functions of the foot and leg tendons and muscles. By applying some of the laws of biomechanics, it is possible to come up with accurate descriptions of what takes place in the running stride and of the role each key joint action plays. This is one of the key features I have included in this book that applies to all running styles and speeds.

Improving your physical abilities plays the most important role in the development of an effective running style. The more you can improve your physical abilities to run faster or farther, the more effective your run can be. Keep in mind that, regardless of the shoes or clothing you use, you must still be able to run in a particular manner to capitalize on the equipment *and* your physical assets.

I have biomechanically analyzed many of the best runners in the world to determine key joint actions in running and to evaluate the sequence of their occurrence. To be as objective as possible, the key joint actions in the run and when they occurred were identified through high-speed videotaping and frame-by-frame analysis of the tapes. Illustrative photos were selected to identify the major actions, and then special strength, flexibility, and explosive exercises were created to duplicate these actions.

The special exercises duplicate each distinct movement so that strength and flexibility are developed with the same movement and range of motion as in running. In this way, the strength and flexibility you gain from doing the exercises have an immediate and positive effect on your running.

To illustrate: Once you develop an effective forward thigh drive, you will find your stride length increases and you will be in position for a more forceful leg pullback action to give you an even more powerful pushoff. The forward knee drive is one of the key speed-producing actions in running. In sprinting, where it is most forceful, it is possible to see the thigh rise almost to the level position. In marathon running the thigh rises to approximately 45 degrees because of the slower speed and the need

for greater economy (less energy expenditure). In all cases, however, a strong knee drive maximizes stride length and pushoff force.

The muscles involved in driving the thigh forward are the hip flexors, located in front of the hip. A hip exercise involving these muscles in the same action and range of motion strengthens them in the way they are used in the run. As a result you learn the feel of movement as the muscles grow stronger, which in turn enables you to have a more effective thigh drive. The increased levels of strength, flexibility, and speed of movement give you more control of the thigh pathway and increase the amount of power you can generate in your run.

The method used is known as the Yessis method, or the Yessis 3-Step Method. It consists of three overlapping steps that all runners should go through in order to improve their performance. First and foremost is Step 1, improvement of technique. In order to enhance the learning and improvement of technique, specialized strength and flexibility exercises are simultaneously worked on. These exercises duplicate what you must do to learn the correct muscle feel and actions that are involved.

As technique is perfected, additional strength and flexibility exercises are given to improve strength and flexibility and to make technique changes more easily. This is Step 2. As you increase your levels of strength, not only does your technique become more effective and efficient but your running speed improves. In Step 3, your technique and physical abilities are perfected and coupled tightly together. Some aspects of speed are also introduced. At this time you are capable of displaying more effective and efficient technique, which is the basis for further improvement of specific, functional physical abilities. With an increase in your physical abilities specific to your technique, speed automatically increases. The increases are even more significant when some speed work is added to the workouts. As a result you make the fastest progress possible in relation to effective, efficient, and faster running.

By closely examining each key action of the running stride you will gain a better understanding of each movement and how the specialized exercises can improve each action. This knowledge and its application can speed up your improvement greatly.

Unfortunately, it takes an injury before most individuals begin to see the true value of doing exercises specific to running.

Henry is a classic example. He was involved in a car accident and had severe back and shoulder problems. I helped him out with exercises specific to his injuries and introduced some special exercises to help him in his running. At first he was a nonbeliever and only did the exercises for his back and shoulder. However, as he began to see positive results he slowly began to incorporate the running exercises into his routine. It wasn't long before he saw dramatic results in his running. Not only was he able to run farther, but he felt much stronger when running. According to him, the run was becoming effortless.

Henry continued his exercises for about three to four months and before long became a proficient runner. He is firmly convinced the exercises played a major role in his recovery and in the overall improvement of his running. He now has many other runners in his club doing some of these exercises and is a strong believer that only through proper physical training can runners realize their true potential.

By studying the illustrations of the running actions and the specialized exercises, you will have a better understanding of how each of these exercises relates to your personal running. If your running technique deviates greatly from the norm on the actions presented, then you should modify your technique and some of the exercises to fit your run. Doing these simple exercises on a weekly basis will give you the necessary strength, flexibility, and speed of movement required to execute the proper mechanics of running and to run faster and farther than ever before.

The improvement resulting from these exercises can often be quite dramatic. I recently began working with a young high school runner who had good running times but was not exceptional. In the Southern California area he ranked in the top 100 or 200 runners in the 100-, 200-, and 400-yard runs.

To start, I analyzed his technique and prescribed a specific strength-training program to develop the muscles needed to improve his technique, enhance his running, and produce harmonious muscle development.

He worked religiously on the exercises and after about four months we began fine-tuning technique and getting into speed and explosive training in preparation for the track season. He did well in the 100-, 200-, and 400-yard runs but still was not exceptional. After the season he began working very hard on strength training, and slowly incorporated explosive training. We did not do any all-out speed training.

The best time he had during the track season was more than eleven seconds in the 100-yard run. In the three to four months after the conclusion of the track season, he did strength and explosive training together with some running to incorporate the changes in technique and in his physical abilities. In this way, the changes were hardly noticed and the running became smoother and more effortless. Since he was going to go out for football, I timed him in the 40-yard dash just before the tryouts. His time was 4.5 seconds. To check this we did some repeat 40s, all of which fell within the 4.5- to 4.6-second range.

The improvement was outstanding in view of the fact that he did not do any running-speed work. He worked mainly on form running to perfect his technique and his physical abilities. Because of the improvement in his physical abilities he was able to decrease his times appreciably without doing an excessive amount of running, which typically overloads the muscles and leads to injury. For him this is just the beginning. He has much more room for improvement in his technique and physical abilities!

The same can happen to you. By doing the exercises that duplicate what you do in running you will be able to develop the strength, flexibility, and explosiveness needed to improve your times greatly, much more so than if you only ran.

2

Develop Strength and Flexibility

The main goal of a specialized strength and flexibility exercise program is to improve your ability to efficiently execute the key joint actions in running. This in turn maximizes your running distance, speed, and economy. The special strength and flexibility exercises presented in this book will enhance and improve your run in a shorter period than if you doubled your running time! Specifically, greater strength and flexibility will enable you to more easily perform the following key elements of the running stride:

1. Maintain a Balanced Posture While Running. With increased strength of the leg, hip, and trunk muscles, you can more easily maintain a balanced posture throughout the entire run. This enables you to have more powerful leg movements and increases your ability to control your limb movements in the run.

2. Hold the Back (Spine) in an Erect, Safe Position. By strengthening the lower-back and hip-extensor muscles, you can maintain the trunk with normal spinal curvature in the lower back during the entire run. When the spine is at its normal curvature, shearing and compression forces on the disks are reduced

greatly. This in turn allows you to run safely, especially when running faster or for longer distances. With the spine in good position, your leg actions become even more effective.

3. Demonstrate Active Flexibility. Runners are often advised to use static stretching in which they hold a position for about twenty to thirty seconds. Such stretching is recommended to prevent injury, and as a warm-up. However, contrary to popular belief, it has never been proved that static stretches prevent injury! The number of injuries are the same regardless of whether you do such stretches. Also, since static stretches are not functional, they do not raise body temperature or physically prepare the muscles for action—yet these are the main purposes of stretching in a warm-up.

Your joints must have the needed range of motion, or flexibility, to ensure a full range of limb movements. But your muscles must provide the force for these movements, as well as joint stability, throughout the total range of motion. If you have unstable joints—which occur when ligaments and tendons are overstretched and muscles are not strong enough to maintain joint integrity—you are highly prone to injury.

Running is dynamic, not static, so doing static stretches for greater flexibility is not specific to running. To make your stretches more functional, you should do active stretches that prepare the muscles for action and enable you to develop strength with flexibility. Keep in mind that the strength of the muscles moves the limbs through the range of motion needed in running. Having great flexibility does not guarantee or have any relation to the ability of the muscles to move you through this range of motion. In other words, static flexibility has no correlation to the active movements seen in running. However, developing both strength and flexibility in the same exercise saves time and is very specific to running. This is the natural way to stretch and strengthen the muscles and joints to see positive changes in the shortest amount of time.

4. Increase Running Speed and Distance. When you increase the strength of the muscles involved in running, you can move the legs and arms faster and more forcefully and with higher levels of coordination. As a result, you can generate greater speed. Because strength is related to speed of movement, the greater your strength levels, the faster and more forcefully you can move the limbs, but only up to a certain point. In addition to strength, runners need speed strength—strength coupled with speed. This is the key to quick, fast, and explosive running.

5. Improve Control of Body Movements. Control of body movement is related to neuromuscular coordination, a key element in effective running. Running technique involves integrating the nervous and muscular systems to control the limb and body movements. Part of neuromuscular coordination is muscle strength—not maximum strength but sufficient strength to enable the movements to be executed safely and effectively. Understand that coordination consists of contracting the muscles with the needed intensity, with the right timing, and in the correct sequence. By doing the recommended specialized strength exercises, you will enhance coordination.

6. Develop a Muscular Feel. Most runners who have run for any substantial period of time are familiar with the muscular feel for the joint actions. This muscular feel is a key factor in improving and perfecting your running technique. If you need improvement in a key action of the running stride, then you must practice the particular movement to develop the neuromuscular pathway until it feels natural.

By doing a strength exercise that duplicates a specific action, you not only learn the feel of the movement sooner, but you also increase control of the movement. As a result, it is much easier to incorporate the new or modified action into the total run. Once the new movement is mastered, you will have a good feel for it. I have worked with many runners who have difficulty pulling the leg backward after the forward knee drive. By doing specialized exercises, such as the straight-leg pulldown in which rubber tubing provides the resistance, this problem is corrected. When you learn the feel of the pullback action, it enables you to incorporate the movement more easily and, as a result, create greater power in the pushoff.

7. Learn Running Technique. The need for strength to learn how to run effectively or to learn the key running actions is evident when first attempting new or different movements. For example, you need adequate strength of the lower-back muscles to hold your trunk erect. You need adequate strength of the thigh (quadriceps) muscles to prevent "sitting" after touchdown, and hip muscle strength to drive the thigh forward and backward. If you do not have the strength to carry out these actions, you cannot learn to execute the specific actions needed in effective running. You develop a poor or even potentially dangerous running pattern. Remember, the run you develop is determined to a great extent by your physical capabilities.

8. Change Running Technique. The two basic ways of improving your running are through more effective technique and increased physical capabilities. If a particular change in technique is needed and you do not have the physical ability to make the change, you will not be able to improve your running. For example, if you do not have sufficient midsection muscle strength you will be unable to keep your hips and shoulders from rotating excessively. I can relate many other examples showing how specific exercises enable you to achieve the modifications desired. But suffice it to say that developing your physical abilities, especially strength and flexibility, plays the critical role in shaping your run, and helping you run faster and farther.

9. Develop Muscular Endurance. By increasing strength you can also improve muscular endurance. This is done by increasing the number of repetitions in the strength exercise so that you will be able to run farther without discomfort or fear of injury. Greater muscular endurance will also enable you to maintain proper running form throughout the distance. In addition, it is the key to running longer for greater aerobic (cardiovascular and respiratory) endurance.

10. Prevent Injury. Effective technique, together with adequate flexibility, muscle strength, and strong tendons and ligaments, can prevent injury. If the limbs and joints are well stabilized and under control when the running forces are encountered, the chances of injury are minimal. In such cases, the muscles and support structures can safely withstand the forces. If your body movements are uncoordinated or uncontrolled when you run, the muscles, tendons, and ligaments have little margin for error. As a result, they may become stretched or torn when sufficiently fatigued or if the forces are exceptionally high.

Efficient running demands considerable skill, a full range of motion, and the necessary muscular force to execute key joint actions in the shoulders, arms, hips, knees, feet, and ankles. Having adequate levels of strength and flexibility, coupled with good technique, will decrease the number of injuries and greatly enhance your run.

Almost all runners experience some physical problems in their running years, often due to excess running. This comes from the general recommendation that if you want to become a better runner you must run more. But increasing your running distance or speed without first physically preparing yourself can lead to overuse injuries because of the additional stress on the muscles and joints. Do not be fooled into thinking that you are also improving strength and flexibility if your distance improves from extra running. Your strength remains the same, which creates an imbalance because of greater

aerobic development. The end result is an injury when your strength levels can no longer handle the joint and muscle stresses.

11. Speed Up Rehabilitation. Greater strength aids in rehabilitation. If you happen to get injured and already have adequate strength levels, you will find you recover faster. In addition, strength training is one of the primary methods used in rehabilitating injuries. Muscular activity as an aid in medical restoration lies in the development of strength, endurance, flexibility, skill, and relaxation. These elements are basic to successful recovery as well as to running.

12. Breathe More Efficiently. Breathing plays an important role in running and relaxation. When your respiratory muscles are strong, you are capable of taking in and processing more air per breath. As a result, you can get greater amounts of oxygen, which the body needs for energy production and to help in recovery.

The stronger your respiratory muscles, the more effective your cardiovascular endurance. By improving the strength of the muscles involved in breathing, you will be able to prevent the onset of fatigue and recover faster. Keep in mind that respiratory fatigue occurs before cardiovascular fatigue. Thus your breathing is directly related to your endurance.

13. Improve Aerobic Capabilities. Strength is closely related to the development of aerobic capabilities. Too often, aerobic training is erroneously considered the best or only way to prepare yourself physically for running. There is no doubt that improving your aerobic abilities will enhance your overall running, but it must be supplemented with other training.

When you engage in aerobic conditioning (or in cross-training activities such as cycling, swimming, rowing, or other cyclical and continuous activities), your cardiovascular and respiratory functions improve. But strength does not increase! As a result, after you engage in aerobic activity for a period of time, you develop an imbalance between your aerobic capabilities and your strength levels, which can lead to injury. By developing greater muscle strength, however, you will be able to do aerobic activities more effectively and with less chance of injury.

14. Slow Down the Aging Process. Strength training is especially beneficial in slowing the aging process. Many runners are already middle age or older and anticipate running as long as possible. In order to do this, however, they need adequate strength, flexibility, and other physical abilities. Most individuals lose strength as they age, but the main reason for this is that they do not do supplementary strength-training exercises to maintain the levels they had in their youth.

It is never too late to gain strength. Individuals in their seventies and eighties are capable of doubling their strength within a matter of weeks! Some people run their first marathon in their eighties! By maintaining or increasing your strength and other physical qualities, you will not notice many of the drastic changes typically associated with old age.

Many runners can run fairly well, mainly because of consistency and constant practice. In spite of physical losses, they are still capable of executing consistent, if not powerful, runs. However, as you begin to lose physical qualities, injuries become more prevalent and running technique becomes more erratic. Thus it is extremely important, especially for seniors, to maintain and increase strength, flexibility, balance, and coordination levels to continue to have the best run possible.

15. Develop Confidence. As you improve your technique or increase strength and flexibility, your confidence in being able to perform as needed improves greatly. Confidence is based on your ability to execute whatever the task may be. The more capable you are of executing the key actions involved in running, the more confidence you will have in being able to maintain good technique and cover the distance without any problems. With greater confidence in your abilities you will be better prepared for racing as well as increasing running speed and distance.

General Strength Exercises

General strength exercises are those exercises used in overall body conditioning. They are not directly related to the specific actions seen in running, for example, strengthening the muscles as they are used in running and increasing your functional potential for running. The overhead press exercise can be used to illustrate the concept of a general strength exercise. It is a common exercise used in fitness programs in which the arms move directly upward in a sideward pattern. In running, however, the arms move in a forward-backward motion below the shoulder in relation to the trunk. Thus, the overhead press is a good exercise for strengthening the shoulders and arms, which are used in running, but it is not directly related to how you run.

Specialized Strength Exercises

When the movement pattern in the exercise duplicates what occurs in the run, it is known as a specialized exercise. An example of a specialized exercise for the shoulders is driving your arm from behind your body to in front of your body in the same pathway and in the same range of motion as seen in the running stride.

The key to improving your performance is to do special exercises that duplicate the movements and actions seen in the actual run. Developing physical abilities specific to running will have the greatest impact on improving your ability to run more efficiently, and faster and longer.

Specialized exercises that promote psychological traits consist of movements and actions that require decisiveness, willpower, perseverance, and confidence to achieve specific goals. They have similar concentration and psychological qualities as seen during the run, especially in a race. For example, execution of certain specialized exercises requires concentration to develop the neuromuscular pathway needed. A strength exercise duplicating one aspect of the stride requires ultimate concentration and perseverance to repeat exactly the same movement time after time to develop the necessary muscle feel. For specialized exercises to have maximum positive transfer, you must be decisive in your movements and actions in order to develop the confidence to repeat the action during the run.

Criteria for Specialized Strength Exercises

For an exercise to be specific it must fulfill one or more of the following criteria:

1. The exercise must duplicate the exact movement witnessed in certain actions of the running stride, such as an exercise duplicating the exact ankle, knee, hip, or shoulder action.

2. The exercise must involve the same type of muscular contraction used in the actual run. For example, in the sprinting pushoff, the muscles undergo an explosive shortening contraction (after being pre-tensed) to produce maximum force and resultant running speed. After the initial contraction the limb continues on its own momentum until the antagonist muscles undergo a strong lengthening (eccentric) contraction to slow down and stop the limb before an injury can occur. Thus the special exercise must include an explosive muscular contraction as occurs in the joint action.

3. The special exercise must have the same range of motion as in the actual run. Doing an exercise with the arms raised above the head and then pulling them downward may use the same muscles but not the same range of motion needed in the arm action. More specific is to move the arm backward and upward so that it duplicates the exact range of motion in which strength is applied.

The concept of exercise specificity is new to running but the term *specificity* is not. Many authors have used the term *specific exercises* but few exercises actually fulfilled the previously mentioned criteria. The specificity referred to by these authors usually refers to strengthening or stretching the muscles that may be involved, but not in the way they are used in the running stride.

Running uphill to develop strength is a classic example of a general exercise considered specific to running. Raising the thighs when running uphill is not in the same range of action and omits the important initial explosive contraction of the hip flexors. In addition, the ankle extension drives the body upward rather than forward. This ankle action can still be of benefit but, because of the need to drive the knees up, it plays a secondary role to leg extension. In running, ankle extension is a primary force, knee extension is not.

Typical strength and conditioning programs for runners deal with general exercises to get you "in shape." In some cases, the exercises that are prescribed use the same muscles used in running. But if these exercises do not duplicate the same range of motion, the same type of muscle contraction, or the exact movement and coordination seen in running, they will not directly improve the run.

Researchers who have done electromyographic studies to determine the muscular involvement in running found that the abdominals play a major role. To strengthen the abdominals the researchers recommended the crunch and the crunch with a twist. These exercises do, of course, strengthen the abdominals, but only through a very small range of motion that is not specific to the run. More specifically, when the abdominals come into play, it is mainly the abdominal oblique muscles that are used to prevent the hips and shoulders from rotating too much during the run. The obliques also play a major role in maintaining a firm connection between the leg and arm action.

The crunch, or sit-up, mainly strengthens the upper abdominals. In running, especially in sprinting, only the lower abdominals play an important role. The crunch with a twist involves the obliques but the range of motion is extremely small and, more important, the twisting occurs when the spine is flexed. This is potentially dangerous since trunk rotation should always take place when the spine is maintained in its normal curvature. Even though the exercises strengthen the abdominals they are not specific to the actual muscle actions involved in running. In addition, greater upper-abdominal strength can lead to poor posture while running by pulling down the chest and shoulders.

For maximum effectiveness, strength development must be synchronized with your running to ensure it is usable strength, or strength that can be displayed in your running. This is the value specialized exercises can give you that general exercises cannot.

Because of the need for skill duplication, most exercises are best done with elastic tubing, such as in the Active Cords set, especially for the leg, hip, and shoulder actions. The Active Cords set that I developed consists of three elastic cords with different tensions with a swivel clip at each end for easy connections as needed for various exercises. Also included is a special nonslip hip belt to which the rubber tubing can be attached at different locations to create different effects. There are two handles for pulling actions, an ankle belt for leg and hip exercises, and a dual attachment for use in a door or for attachment to any beam or post. A dual attachment adjustable strap for stretching back and shoulder muscles and doing pullups is optional. It is very difficult, and in some cases impossible, to duplicate the exact movements of the legs, hips, and shoulders with dumbbells, barbells, or machines. Also important are medicine ball and dumbbell exercises for other exercises that cannot be done with rubber tubing.

Proper Breathing During Specialized Exercises

When you exercise, your breathing is very important, therefore you should develop proper breathing patterns from the start. This also applies to running.

The instructions for the exercises tell you to inhale and to hold your breath on exertion—that is, on the hardest part of the exercise, when you are overcoming resistance. You then exhale on the return, staying in control of the movements. But don't be surprised if you read or hear the opposite from other sources—that you should exhale on exertion and inhale on return.

The widely used recommendation to exhale on exertion is based on theory, not research, and applies mainly to people with heart and circulatory system problems. For example, if you hold your breath for too long (up to eight seconds with a maximal exertion), you could pass out. That is because the internal pressure in the chest and abdomen increases when you hold your breath on exertion. If it increases greatly, it squeezes down on the blood vessels shuttling blood and oxygen to and from the heart. When this happens, you can black out (but rarely, and only on maximum exertion).

If you are without cardiovascular problems and do not hold your breath for more than a few seconds as needed in the recommended exercises, the breath-holding on exertion is perfectly safe. It makes the exercises safer and more effective. If you have high blood pressure or other circulatory system or heart problems, avoid heavy resistance and breath-holding.

Inhaling and holding the breath briefly on exertion—any exertion, in all sports, including running—comes naturally. Many studies have shown that whenever athletic skills are executed properly, athletes hold their breath on the exertion—during the power phase—when maximum force is generated. The breath-holding is especially important in the running stride pushoff and touchdown.

Inhaling and holding the breath on exertion provide up to 20 percent greater force, stabilize the spine, and prevent lower-back injuries. They transform the trunk (and, in fact, the whole body) into a stable unit against which your hips, shoulders, and arms can move more effectively.

The need to hold your breath when doing heavy lifting can be inferred from the recommendations given for relaxation. In order to relax, you are told to inhale and then exhale. As you exhale, you relax the muscles. In essence, exhalation is associated with relaxation. Therefore is it wise to exhale when you are lifting a heavy weight? Actually, it is natural to hold your breath in this situation. Watch people lifting heavy weights at the gym and you will see that they hold their breath during the exertion. Their cheeks are puffed out, their blood vessels are distended, and their mouths are closed. They are in danger only if they hold their breath too long, that is, double the amount of time taken to do an exercise at a normal, moderate rate of speed.

Breathing exercises can also help you relax before a race. Inhaling and then exhaling before starting a race is a good technique to help you relax. But before starting, it is important that the muscles have some tension—not excessive tension, but sufficient tension to take off with power.

Thus, inhalation and breath-holding are needed immediately before and during execution of the key actions. Studies done with devices to monitor breathing patterns have proved this beyond any doubt. To execute a powerful takeoff, you must hold your breath during execution.

In effective breathing, do not inhale to your maximum capacity and then hold it. Doing this can make you very uncomfortable. Just take a breath slightly greater than usual and then hold it to experience the positive benefits. This is especially important for stabilizing the body, holding the spine in position, and getting greater power in your touchdown and takeoff. Contact time is very short. Thus, you should have no fear of holding your breath too long or of overexerting yourself.

3

The Biomechanics of Running

Biomechanics Explored

The term *biomechanics* is being used with increasing frequency in the sports and fitness fields. It is not uncommon to hear of biomechanically correct running shoes, biomechanically correct exercise machines, and biomechanically correct technique. It is a catchy buzzword but one that few individuals seem to put into practice.

Biomechanics, as used in this book, employs biology (kinesiology), physics (mechanics of running), and engineering concepts. Kinesiological factors are taken into consideration with the mechanical aspects of running, then engineering is used to develop the most efficient model, or to enhance running technique or speed. Thus the biomechanics of running means the technique of running, based on principles of physics, and anatomical and engineering factors.

Through biomechanical study it is possible to determine whether running is efficient in relation to energy utilization and effective in relation to mechanical, kinesiological, and engineering factors. In most cases, efficiency and effectiveness are closely intertwined. However, it must be noted that bio-

mechanical studies and analyses as provided in this book are still quite rare.

Most studies, rather than analyzing each runner in relation to these factors, compare subjects to world-class runners. It is taken for granted that world-class runners have perfect biomechanics or the best technique possible. However, this is often far from true since some runners with major technique flaws also win. (Imagine how good they could be with effective technique!) In addition, with special exercises and training methods, all runners—including world-class performers—can improve their technique and their ability to run faster and farther.

I recently worked with Jose Barbosa, a four-time Olympian in the 800 meters. (See Fig. 3.1.) He has won gold and silver in this event (and in the 1,500 meters) in world-class competition, which testifies to his great abilities. However, after I videotaped him and did a frame-by-frame biomechanical analysis of his technique, I found he was lacking in several major actions.

For speed Barbosa relied on a strong knee drive and pushoff, which created greater stride length—especially in view of his long legs. He was lacking in the pawback action, which is when the leg is driven down and back to make contact with the ground. He also had too much up-and-down motion in his push-off, and did not use his arms and feet to maximum effect. He was surprised to note these deficiencies but elated that, with technique modification, he would be able to run even better. These changes should assist him in his attempt to set a new world record in his fifth Olympic appearance.

When physical qualities are examined in relation to mechanical qualities it becomes possible to more fully evaluate running effectiveness. But assessments must be done on an individual basis. Some generalities apply to all runners since all runners must execute the same key joint actions. But runners must be evaluated on their own merits or, more specifically, in relation to their physical and mechanical makeup and abilities.

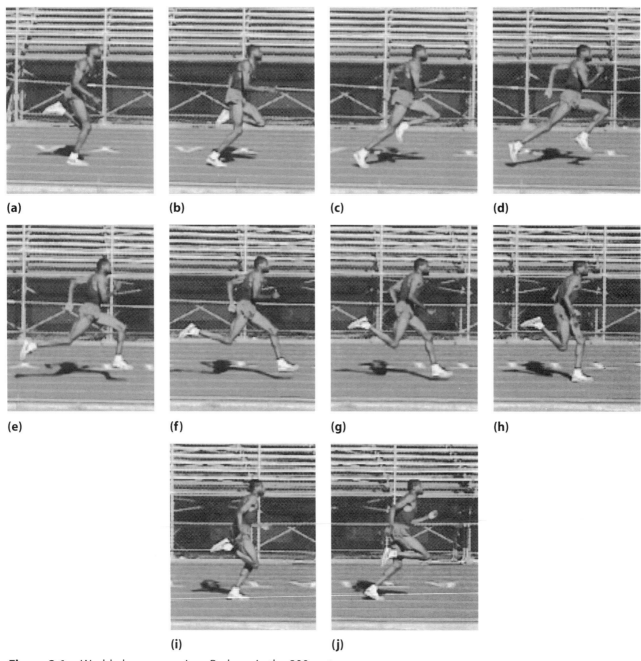

(a) (b) (c) (d)

(e) (f) (g) (h)

(i) (j)

Figure 3.1 World-class runner Jose Barbosa in the 800 meter

Biomechanics is important to runners for two reasons: (1) to improve running performance and (2) to prevent injury. In essence, biomechanics can determine if you are getting the most out of your technique and physical abilities. The greater the effectiveness and efficiency of your running, the greater the benefits to your speed and distance as well as your cardiovascular and respiratory systems. And, the less susceptible you will be to injury.

Biomechanics and Performance

Perusing the theoretical and practical running literature shows that technique is ignored to a great extent, primarily because most coaches and runners believe everyone is born with the ability to run. In addition, it is erroneously believed that running technique should not be changed since individuals will "find" their optimal method and speed. Many coaches firmly believe, "if it works, don't fix it." Fortunately, such thinking does not permeate other fields or we would still be driving Model Ts.

Should running be considered "natural"? Do babies suddenly decide to start running? Of course not! Anyone who has ever raised a child knows it takes a long time before youngsters master the skills of walking and running. Learning to run requires much trial and error before a true movement pattern can be seen. It takes even longer for the running pattern to look smooth and be effective since technique depends on maturity and development of physical qualities. In the early years, strength plays the most important role in developing good technique and increasing running speed.

Since running is not taught in physical education classes, in track or on sports teams, or in running and sports clubs, most people use the trial-and-error method of learning. This is why we see major differences among runners. Some are very smooth, others are jerky; some emphasize only one or two key actions, others involve many extraneous actions. Some runners have a long stride while others have a very short stride. I have even seen runners whose legs never got in front of their bodies!

In this chapter I discuss various aspects of running technique, and have included specific photo frames depicting many of the issues addressed. These frames are taken from videotapes of sprinters and long-distance runners who specialize in different events. (Complete frame-by-frame shots of each runner are included at the end of the chapter in Figs. 3.28–3.41.) All are competitive runners, ranging from regional sprinting champions to top marathon runners, and have achieved some outstanding successes. I purposely avoided including photos of runners with very poor technique.

But even though they are top runners in their particular regions and have strong, positive aspects to their technique, these athletes also have actions that need correction or improvement in order to make their running more efficient. After seeing their films, these runners could not believe many of the things they were doing and told me no one had ever before seriously looked at their technique.

In the animal kingdom it is hard to see major differences in technique among members of the same species. For humans, however, even though some basic skills may be innate (genetics accounts for about one-third of your abilities), the total skill must be learned and perfected in the environment.

Biomechanics plays an extremely important role in improving your running performance. If you are a sprinter, you can easily increase your speed in the 40- and 100-meter dashes by tenths of a second. If you are a long-distance runner, you can increase your running speed in the 5K and 10K by many seconds and even minutes and, in the marathon, by many minutes. In most cases, you can achieve greater speed and greater distance.

Biomechanics and Injury

When you have good running technique, you have good coordination—the ability to contract the muscles at the right time, in the right sequence, and with the right intensity. As a result your movements are smooth and effective. But if technique is poor muscles may contract with excessive force or at the wrong time or in the wrong sequence, which can interfere greatly with your movement coordination and cause injury. In fact, studies indicate that a high percentage of running injuries is due to improper technique.

For example, if you are a heel hitter and land with the sole of your foot angled upward, you will experience braking forces on each touchdown. This means that every time your heel hits the ground it brakes your forward momentum and can generate extremely high forces—from two to ten times body weight depending on the angle of the foot at contact and the speed of running. In general, the greater the angle of the foot when the heel hits the ground and the greater the speed of running, the greater the forces generated. You will find it is impossible to run barefoot with a heel hit because of the high landing forces.

Because the heel hit is erroneously considered "natural," shoe companies make running shoes with a well-cushioned heel to absorb the landing forces. From a biomechanical standpoint this cushioning (and the heel hit) is not only very inefficient but works against the natural muscle and tendon functions. In fact, some recent studies on running shoes indicate they may be a major culprit in running injuries!

With a change in technique to eliminate the heel hit so that you land more mid-foot, you can eliminate most braking forces. You will increase your speed with the resulting more effective pushoff, longer stride length, and diminished braking forces. In addition, running will feel easier and more comfortable.

Because landing forces are decreased greatly when you have a quick ball-heel transition or mid-foot landing, world-class sprinters who have good running technique throw the arm downward as the foot comes in contact with the ground. This increases the landing forces, which are then returned as usable energy during the pushoff. This energy return is also seen in long-distance runners with good technique. They make effective use of the resilient tendons to give back energy rather than relying on the muscles to first absorb landing forces and then generate new forces for the pushoff.

To become a better runner or to simply become more fit for running, the prevalent philosophy is to run more, especially on a more intense level. This is why many runners practice only running on a year-round basis. For example, in preparing for sprints, runners typically do multiple sets of sprints at varying distances. This includes running 40s, 60s, 100s, 150s, 200s, and so on. To participate in a marathon, runners follow a prescribed running schedule of increased mileage. To participate in a 5K or 10K race, runners usually include some long-distance running, sprinting, Fartlek (training that involves changing speed and direction to add fun and creativity to a workout), interval training, and uphill running. Regardless of the running event, the training involves increased running, including hills.

Such an approach leads to injuries. This is why on any given day it is not uncommon to find 25 to 50 percent of all runners not running because of injury. Similar data applies to performers in other aerobic sports such as rowing, cycling, and swimming. To reduce the number of injuries, many runners now cross-train by participating in several aerobic sports. This is only a partial answer to the problem since cross-training does not directly improve performance. It merely helps prevent injury because it changes the way muscles are used while still improving or maintaining aerobic capabilities.

Although weight training is sometimes considered another cross-training sport to prevent injury, it should be classified as supplemental training since its main purpose is to improve performance. Injury prevention should be secondary in weight training.

When you participate in a strength-training program it takes at least six to eight weeks before any true physiological changes occur in the muscles. Earlier gains in strength are due to neuromuscular learning, and improved intra- and inter-muscular coordination. Most important here is to recall that many running injuries are not due to lack of strength, but to poor neuromuscular coordination.

For many years runners have relied more on the quantity of running rather than quality of running. However, by taking a little time to improve the quality of your running, you will be able to go faster and farther but your chances of injury will be diminished.

General Running Technique

Although there are some major differences in running technique from the sprints to the marathon (mainly because of different speeds), the general characteristics are the same. Most technique differences are due to the greater force and range of motion generated in sprinting compared to long-distance running.

In both sprinting and long-distance running the body is basically erect. A distinct forward lean occurs only when accelerating. The chest is slightly raised and the head is held naturally, with the eyes focused in front. The arms and wrists are relaxed, with the elbows bent approximately 90 degrees in long-distance running. Some runners bend and straighten the arms in synchronization with the legs. The arms move forward and back but the hands do not cross the midline.

In sprinting, the thigh rises closer to the level position and touchdown is more directly under the body's center of gravity. Touchdown is on the whole foot or ball to heel. In exceptionally strong sprinters, touchdown is on the ball of the foot only. Approximately 145 to 160 degrees separate the thighs in the flight phase immediately after the pushoff, and actions between the arms and legs are closely coordinated.

In long-distance running, the knee rises to approximately 45 degrees from the vertical and touchdown is slightly in front of the body, close to the center of gravity. Touchdown is on the whole foot or ball-heel. Approximately 90 degrees separate the thighs in the flight phase, and there is smooth, coordinated action between the arms and legs.

In running at speeds in between sprints and long distances, the angle of spread between the thighs is between 100 and 145 degrees and the leg rises to about a 60-degree horizontal angle.

Running Specifics

Before getting into the precise details of running technique, it must be pointed out that it is rare to find a runner with perfect technique. Outstanding runners have very strong positive aspects to their technique, which typically enable them to become winners. The photographs in this book feature some of the best runners in Southern California, but none of them can be used to illustrate each positive aspect of the most effective running technique for either sprints or long distances.

I have looked at the techniques of thousands of runners and have worked with many of them regardless of whether they ran track or were on a team in which they had to run, for example, in football, baseball, lacrosse, or soccer. I have concluded that every runner, regardless of ability, can improve.

Running technique can best be described in three phases: (1) pushoff, (2) flight, and (3) support. In addition, it is possible to distinguish preparation for each of these phases in the preceding phase. For example, in the support phase there is preparation for the pushoff, in the flight phase there is preparation for touchdown, and in the pushoff phase there is preparation for flight.

Pushoff

The pushoff involves one major joint action—ankle-joint extension. The greater the ankle-joint extension, the greater the forward driving force that can be generated.

In the pushoff you push your hips (where your mass is concentrated) forward, rather than pushing your head and shoulders forward, which causes a forward lean. As a result you maintain erect trunk position in which it is possible to see a slight arching (hyperextension) in the lumbar spine. In essence, the hips get pushed in front of the shoulders. As the ankle-joint extension takes place in the pushoff leg, the knee remains slightly bent. (See Fig. 3.2.) If the pushoff (support) leg straightened fully you would be leaping, not running!

All too often, athletes and coaches recommend full leg extension in the pushoff, believing this is the main force-producing action. But straightening the leg fully gives you more of a vertical, rather than a horizontal, force component. The more horizontally the forces are applied, the faster the

Figure 3.2 In pushoff, trunk position is erect and pushoff leg is slightly bent.

running speed. In addition, full leg extension requires more energy, which is wasted on up-and-down motion.

During the pushoff, the hip-extensor muscles (gluteus maximus, hamstrings) do not contract to push you forward. They actually undergo some relaxation and lengthening to keep your center of gravity level as you run. Their main role at this time is to maintain the pelvis and the pushoff leg as a unit. During support they control the amount of bending in the hip joint.

Because the anterior hip-joint ligaments, together with the hip-flexor muscles, prevent the leg from moving behind the body, the pelvic girdle must rotate forward to allow the leg to move behind the body. This shows up in a slight arching of the lumbar spine or, in some runners, as a forward lean—especially if they have tight hip flexors. The hip extensors act mainly as stabilizers at this time.

In the early stages of the pushoff, the swing-leg thigh continues to be driven forward forcefully. The initial forceful contraction of the hip-flexor muscles occurs when the leg is behind the body after the pushoff. The thigh moves on momentum after the pushoff and rises up to about a 75- to 90-degree angle to the body in sprinting (see Fig. 3.3) and about a 45-degree angle in long-distance running (see Fig. 3.4). The more forceful the initial muscular contraction and the knee drive with the pushoff, the higher the thigh rises and the greater the speed at which the shin whips forward.

The knee drive is a key force-producing action that contributes to great speed. The forceful forward swing action of the thigh produces a longer stride length and, as a result, greater speed. To be most effective, however, the forward drive of the swing-leg thigh must begin when the leg is behind the body. The key hip-joint action consists of dri-

(a)

(b)

Figure 3.3 Leg rises to about a 75- to 90-degree angle in sprinting.

Figure 3.4 Leg rises to about 45 degrees in long-distance running.

ving the knee or thigh forward, not upward. The thigh moves upward at the end of the swing-leg forward driving action from the momentum it receives after the pushoff. The greater the force in driving the thigh forward, the faster the thigh comes forward and the faster your potential speed. In long-distance running, however, the pushoff is not as forceful as in sprinting (which also conserves energy) and thus the thigh, in the best marathon runners, only rises to approximately 45 degrees.

The thigh drive can be explained by physics, more specifically, by Newton's First Law of Motion, which states that when a body is placed in motion it will continue in motion until acted upon by some outside force. Thus, in the pushoff when the leg is behind the body and the hip-flexor muscles are pretensed, they can contract explosively to force the thigh forward and then relax as the thigh continues to move forward on its momentum. The hamstring muscles, which are stretched as the leg comes forward, develop tension to control and eventually stop the movement.

As the thigh is driven forward, the shin "folds up" under the thigh so that you drive only the thigh forward, not the entire (extended) leg. Think of the leg as a system of levers, one lever from the hip joint to the knee and one from the knee to the ankle. To bring the leg forward as quickly as possible, which is

needed for speed, it is important to have the shortest lever possible. To produce a short lever, the shin folds under the thigh so the leg is shortened. As a result, you drive only the thigh forward. (See Fig. 3.5.) If you instead swing a fully extended leg forward, it will take much longer.

To prepare for touchdown, the shin swings out to create a long lever that slows the leg. (See Fig. 3.6.) The straight leg is then used to create more force when the leg is driven down and back to make contact with the ground. Each leg action has a specific role and is directly related to the next action in the total sequence.

To ensure there is the shortest lever possible when the shin swings out, it is important that you raise the toe part of the foot. If you follow the swing leg from the time it breaks contact with the ground (See Fig. 3.7.), you can see the foot in plantar flexion (foot extended). Then, as it is getting ready for the shin swing-out and during the swing-out, the foot is dorsi flexed (toe raised). (See Fig. 3.6.) This produces faster leg straightening so that when the leg is brought back it can land more under the body on the ball of the foot or mid-foot. If you kept the toes pointed it would take longer to swing the leg out and you would make contact with the ground too soon, well in front of the body instead of closer to the vertical projection of the center of gravity. The dorsi flexion plays a very important role for speed of the shin's forward movement and ensuring an effective landing.

To better understand the speed of the leg levers do the following: Hold your forearm in place and then bring your hand as far back as possible (hyperextend the wrist). Then whip the hand forward (wrist flexion). As you will see, your hand moves quickly, through about 160 degrees—a key reason you can't see what a magician does since "the hand is quicker than the eye." Now straighten your arm or hold a long pole in your extended arm. Move your arm all the way out to the side and then across the body as fast as possible through the same range of motion. The arm movement now is much slower because of the additional lever length. (If you can find a sufficient light pole, use only the wrist action to see the difference in speed.)

Figure 3.5 Shin folds under thigh to produce a short lever that brings the leg forward quickly.

Figure 3.6 Shin swings out in preparation for touchdown.

The shorter the lever, the faster it can be moved. But the longer the lever, the greater the force at the end of the lever. For example, if you were hit with only a hand in action, you would not feel much force. But an extended arm moving as fast as possible (but slower than the hand alone) can generate so much force at its end that it can do severe damage when contact is made. Because of this, a short lever is great for speed but a long lever is needed for force. In running you satisfy both these conditions by having a short lever to drive the thigh forward and a long lever to bring the leg down for contact.

In regard to economy it is important to note that the shin does not fold up completely behind the

Figure 3.7 Toe is raised to ensure short lever when shin swings out.

thigh. Most important here is that the shin be behind the length of the thigh (between two perpendicular-to-the-thigh lines, one at the knee and one at the hip). This is why for most marathon runners it is possible to see the shin slightly above level as the thigh is brought forward. (See Fig. 3.8.) Keeping the shin basically level saves energy because the hamstring muscles do not have to contract to raise the shin higher. Note also that the shin must be sufficiently high so that the foot can be "hidden" behind the length of the thigh.

In sprinting, because of the greater forces generated, the heel rises higher so that it comes close to the buttocks when the knee is in front of the body. (See Fig. 3.9.) However, since the key action at this time is the knee drive you should still have more of a horizontal, rather than vertical, positioning of the shin during the drive.

Immediately prior to breaking contact with the ground at the end of the pushoff phase, there is full ankle-joint extension and you are on tiptoe. As soon as contact with the ground is broken, the pushoff leg, which now becomes the swing leg, continues its backward movement and knee-joint flexion occurs. You are now in the flight phase. (See Fig. 3.7.)

Note that you do not kick yourself in the butt as is often recommended, especially in sprinting. When the heel gets close to the buttocks, the knee should be in front of the body (as a consequence of the forward knee drive), rather than pointing down toward the ground. Folding the leg, coupled with the knee drive, is very safe. It allows the hamstrings to relax while the hip flexors do the work. If you keep the thigh vertical and kick your butt, the hamstrings will be working when they should be relaxing. This leads to hamstring pulls! In addition, the butt kick slows you down because of the time it takes you to do this instead of driving the thigh forward. For some reason, however, the butt kick has become an accepted practice in many coaching circles.

In working with several high school sprinters, I noticed that the runners kicked themselves in the butt. With stop-action videotape analysis it was pos-

(a)

(b)

Figure 3.8 In long-distance runners, shin is slightly above level as thigh comes forward.

(a)

(b)

Figure 3.9   In sprinting, heel comes close to buttocks when knee is in front of body.

sible to see that their thighs were vertical when their heels were next to the buttocks. When asked if they *practiced* the butt kick, the answer was affirmative. However, the better runners (both sprinters and long-distance runners) focused on driving the knee forward to increase their speed. When the runners who used the butt kick modified their technique to the knee drive, an increase in speed became quite noticeable. Beware of the butt kick as well as the quadriceps stretch, which duplicates the butt kick. This stretch can be detrimental to the knee joint because of the extreme bone-joint separation in the knee joints.

Flight Phase

Once the foot breaks contact with the ground, you are in flight. In general, the flight phase is about as long as the support phase. If it were longer than the support phase you would be running slower. By getting the foot in contact with the ground more often, more force can be generated to continually drive you forward, but there must be a flight phase to use the force that has been generated in the pushoff and the knee and arm drives.

In the best sprinters, during the flight phase the angle between the thighs is about 150 to 165 degrees,

which also shows the need for great hip-joint flexibility. (See Fig. 3.10.) In long-distance runners, it is about 90 to 100 degrees. (See Fig. 3.11.) As speed increases (as the force of the pushoff and thigh drive increases), the separation between the thighs increases. The slower you go, the less the separation and the less the force produced. The larger the angle, the more it indicates good hip-joint flexibility and a more forceful thigh drive and pushoff, in some cases a strong pawback movement.

Figure 3.10   During the flight phase, angle between thighs is about 150 to 165 degrees in sprinters.

Figure 3.11 In long-distance runners, angle between thighs is about 90 to 100 degrees.

As the swing-leg thigh is driven forward and approaches its highest point, the thigh is slowed and then stopped by contraction of the hamstring muscles. As this occurs, the swing-leg shin whips out. (See Fig. 3.12.) In essence, as the thigh decelerates, the shin accelerates forward until there is basically a straight leg. The thigh should not drop appreciably as the leg straightens. Doing so leads to premature ground contact.

Once straightened, the leg immediately begins moving to the rear in preparation for touchdown. To pull the leg back and down (the pawback) the hamstring muscles, which were just placed on eccentric stretch as the thigh moved forward, con-

tract with great force. At this time the hamstrings and gluteus maximus do their most important work. This is also the point where hamstring injuries often occur when technique is poor.

From physiology we know that when a muscle is placed on stretch it will contract with greater force. The stretching action that occurs when the thigh and shin swing forward enables the hamstrings to contract forcefully. As a result, when the swing leg touches down and becomes the support leg, the upper body is propelled forward.

The pawback movement is another major action that contributes to forward speed. In pawback, after the shin is whipped forward, the leg is straightened and then the entire leg moves backward in a pawing action until contact is made with the ground. (See Fig. 3.13.) In long-distance running, touchdown is slightly in front of the body and is typically on mid-foot. In sprinting, the leg is brought back more forcefully so that touchdown is more directly under the body on the ball of the foot or on mid-foot.

The closer the foot lands to the vertical projection of the body's center of mass, the less the braking force generated. This is the main reason the heel hit is so inefficient in running. When you land on the heel, the leg is well in front of the body so that it momentarily stops your forward motion because of the ground-reaction forces created. These forces, which can be up to ten times your body weight, are the culprits in many of the running injuries that

(a)

(b)

(c)

Figure 3.12 As the hamstring muscles contract, the swing-leg shin whips out.

(a)   (b)   (c)

Figure 3.13   After shin whips forward, leg is straightened, then moves backward.

occur in the foot, ankle, knee, hip, and even lower back. To eliminate the braking forces as much as possible, it is important that the leg be moving backward as it makes contact with the ground.

This backward leg movement and the following touchdown are very important in continuing fast forward movement of the upper body. At ground contact, the upper body can move in front of the support leg so that, when the pushoff occurs, the body will be as far out in front as possible. (See Fig. 3.14.) In this way the pushoff is directed more in a horizontal (forward) line, rather than projecting the body upward, as typically occurs in the heel hit.

Note that in the heel hit when the whole foot comes down to make ground contact it takes longer for the upper body to move over the foot. As a result,

when you push off, the body is not as far forward as possible and you have a strong vertical pushoff component. Because of this, the heel hit prevents you from running at your maximum speed as well as being highly dangerous.

Support Phase

The support phase is used mainly to hold the body upright, to somewhat relax the muscles that were just in action, and to prepare other muscles for the pushoff action. In sprinting, upon ground contact your center of gravity is lowered very little. It is significantly lower in slow distance running, which creates more up-and-down motion. This in turn uses more energy to drive you upward rather than forward. If your support muscles are weak and allow you to sink too much after contact, your run becomes very inefficient.

For example, if you lifted the body higher by even one centimeter in a 5,000-meter run, you would be doing the equivalent of work required to lift your body mass to the height of a five-story building. This is extra work performed in a very uneconomical vertical movement, which has a strong negative influence on your running speed. The more horizontally the body moves, the greater your speed.

World-class sprinters are most adept at running "level." Studies show that their center of gravity oscillates vertically only about an inch. In long-distance

Figure 3.14   On pushoff, the body is far out in front.

running, however, it is often double or triple this amount. This is due to the shorter stride length, the landing taking place more in front of the body, and greater flexion of the support leg. In effective running, the pathway of the center of mass should create a smooth undulating curve, moving down during the support phase and reaching its highest peak during flight. When the vertical rise is sharp, it indicates a more vertical pushoff.

The support phase, also known as the phase of amortization, begins when the foot makes contact with the ground and the leg undergoes some flexion. (See Fig. 3.15.) Once contact is made on the ball of the foot it is followed immediately by the heel, or contact is made on the mid-foot, usually on the outside border of the foot. This latter type of touchdown is made most often by long-distance runners.

At this time the arch of the foot undergoes some depression. (See Fig. 3.16.) This is very important for the initial shock absorption and to tense the muscles and tendons on the plantar surface of the foot. At the same time, the ankle, knee, and hip joints undergo slight flexion to absorb some of the landing forces and, most important, to withstand the landing forces. (See Fig. 3.17.)

When you land ball-heel or mid-foot, the eccentric stretching tenses the foot-arch tendons and the Achilles tendon and calf muscles. In addition, to

(a)   **(b)**

Figure 3.15 The support phase begins when the foot touches down and the leg flexes.

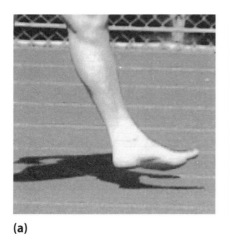
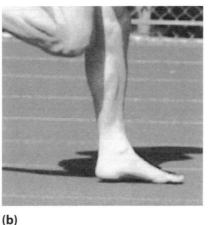
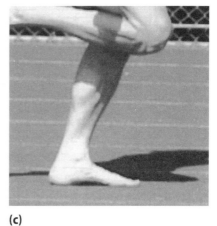

(a)   **(b)**   **(c)**

Figure 3.16 The arch undergoes some depression during contact.

Figure 3.17 At touchdown, ankle, knee, and hip joints flex slightly.

prevent excessive flexion in the knee and hip joints, the knee and hip-extensor muscles contract eccentrically and the built-up tension prevents you from excessively lowering your body. When these muscles are weak you will experience excessive sinking of the body, which leads to a stronger vertical component in the pushoff.

Stretching the Achilles and other tendons is very important for creating energy in the pushoff. Note that stretching this tendon forcefully and quickly leads to greater tension in the tendon and associated muscles. The tension created is needed mainly to withstand the forces of the landing and only partially to absorb them. When all the forces are absorbed there will be no energy to give back in the pushoff. Thus, there should only be enough absorption to prevent injury on initial contact.

The Achilles tendon, one of the longest and strongest tendons in the body, can withstand great tension. When the body weight is over the foot, the tension builds up greatly. Even though some forces are absorbed on landing, most are withstood in the muscle and tendon, which tense in preparation for the pushoff. The tension builds up as the body moves forward so that at the moment of pushoff the energy accumulated is given back as pushoff force when the tendons shorten and muscles contract. In this way the muscles do less work, making the run more efficient.

For example, since the change in length of the calf muscles in effective running (especially sprinting) is minimal, most energy stored in the Achilles tendon is given back as propulsive force. This action economizes on energy and produces greater speed in sprints and speed endurance in long-distance running.

If you did not make contact on mid-foot but instead landed on the heel, the Achilles tendon would not be able to absorb or withstand any of the landing forces. As a result, the forces would travel straight up the body and become dangerous. But with an effective touchdown, the Achilles and foot tendons can perform their normal function of absorbing and withstanding the landing forces and give them back in the pushoff.

Arm Actions

In effective and safe running, arm action must coordinate with leg action. During pushoff and flight, as the knee is driven forward, the arm on the opposite side of the body is also driven forward from a position behind the body. In most runners the arm moves forward in front of the body until the hands are about shoulder high. In addition, the elbow flexes to 90 degrees or less during the forward drive in both sprinting and long-distance running. (See Fig. 3.18.) This is most important for speed of movement to synchronize with the thigh drive. Only in this way can the arm action contribute force to increase speed.

Most long-distance runners maintain the arms at approximately a 90-degree angle from the elbows to economize energy, and the amount of opening and closing of the angle is fairly small. The elbow is raised to the rear during the backswing phase of the arm action, while the opposite arm is brought forward to synchronize with the thigh drive. Note that most of the arm action occurs behind the body. The elbow rises approximately 45 degrees to the rear as it mimics the range of motion in the hip joint.

The arms move basically in a forward-backward motion so that all the driving forces move in a straight line forward. However, note that if your shoulders rotate (turn sideways), your arms may appear to cross the body, though in reality they do not. (See Fig. 3.19.) Thus, if you see your hands coming across your body, check to see if it is due to the shoulder rotation or if your elbows flare out to the sides.

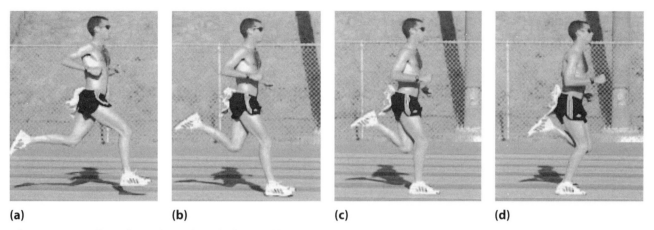

(a)   **(b)**   **(c)**   **(d)**

Figure 3.18   Elbow flexes in both sprinting and long-distance running.

(a)   **(b)**   **(c)**

(d)   **(e)**   **(f)**

Figure 3.19   Arms may appear to cross the body, but do not.

In sprinting, there is a powerful forward drive of the arm as the elbow flexes to 90 degrees or less after being straightened. The arm flexes and moves forward until the elbow is alongside or just slightly in front of the body, there is approximately a 90-degree bend in the elbow, and the hand is about shoulder high. (Note that if the elbow is too far forward the hand will be too high.) The arm then straightens (very forcefully in some sprinters) as it moves back and down so that when the arm is alongside the body it is relatively straight. (See Fig. 3.20.) The long lever of the arm is needed to slow it down so that it synchronizes with the leg stopping when the foot is in contact with the ground.

After the arm straightens, the elbow is then raised to the rear. This action bends the elbow slightly and prepares it for being driven forward in synchronization with the bent-leg forward knee drive. (See Fig. 3.18.) This combination of actions gives you efficient arm movement and contributes to greater speed. Because economy is so important in long-distance running, the arms straighten very little so that they remain bent about 90 degrees.

The arms play a very important role in keeping the shoulders square to the direction of running, which in turn keeps the hips square so the thighs move directly forward and backward. If your hips turn sideways, your foot plant may show a zigzag pattern that directs the pushoff force somewhat to the sides rather than directly forward.

In order for the shoulders and hips to remain square (facing forward), you must have strong abdominal-oblique muscles in addition to strong lower-back muscles, which also maintain your upright position. Your shoulders and neck should be relaxed even when you are striving to run faster and feel increasing fatigue. If these muscles become tense you will be very tight across the neck and shoulders, which not only brings on greater fatigue but restricts effective arm movement.

Front and Rear Views

A biomechanical analysis would not be complete without also looking at the front and rear views of a runner. (See Figs. 3.21 and 3.22.) These views are needed to see some movements that cannot be seen from the side view. For example, are the knees driven directly forward or do they crisscross the body, creating zigzag forces? Do the arms cross the body? Do the feet cross the body during the forward drive of the knee? To answer these and other questions it is necessary to study the front and rear views to see if there are any major deviations to what constitutes good technique.

During the forward knee drive, the knee should be driven directly forward and not out to the side or crossing the midline. In this way you know that all the forces are being directed in a straight line in

(a) **(b)** **(c)** **(d)**

Figure 3.20 In sprinting, the arm flexes, then straightens alongside the body.

Figure 3.21 Front view

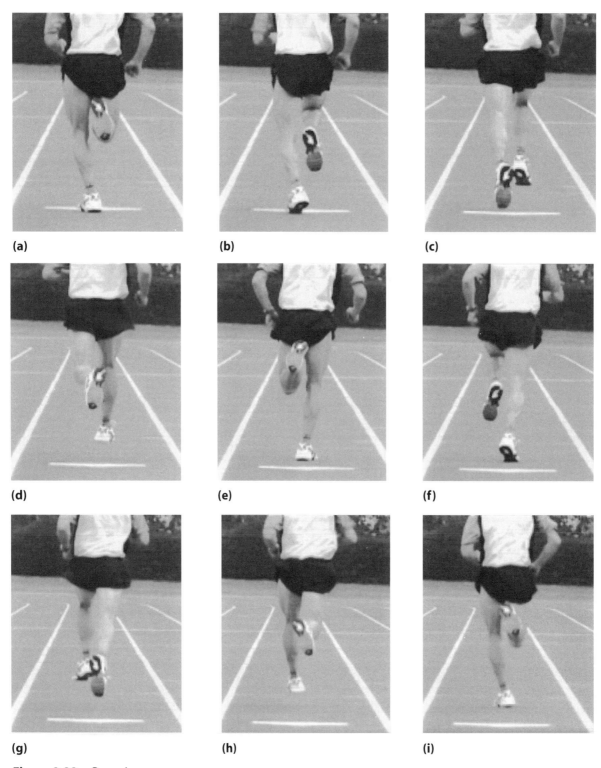

Figure 3.22   Rear view

the direction of the run. This is very important for maximizing forward speed. In addition, the arms should not move excessively to the sides or cross the midline. The rear view is important to see what happens to the feet during the flight phase—for example, if the feet cross the midline or flare out to the sides. If this occurs it usually indicates some hip-joint muscle imbalance. And this view enables you to see if there is excessive pronation or supination of the foot during the support phase. (See Fig. 3.23.)

The front and rear views also make it possible to see if the foot is directly under the head, which shows very good balance during the run. Fig. 3.24 is an example of good balance. In Fig. 3.21, the runner's head is over the support leg but he has a tendency to favor the left side.

Other Important Aspects of Technique

One of the important features of running fast is the forceful forward drive of the thigh. The faster the thigh comes forward, the greater your stride length and the better the preparation for a forceful pawback movement. This makes it possible to complete each stride more quickly, which increases stride frequency. In sprinting, the knee is brought forward at maximum speed so that when ground contact is made with the opposite leg you will see only one thigh when viewed from the side. (See Fig. 3.18.) In other words, the forward moving thigh lines up with the backward moving thigh as full contact with the ground takes place. In some cases the swing leg is driven forward so forcefully it may be slightly in front of the support thigh. (See Fig. 3.25.)

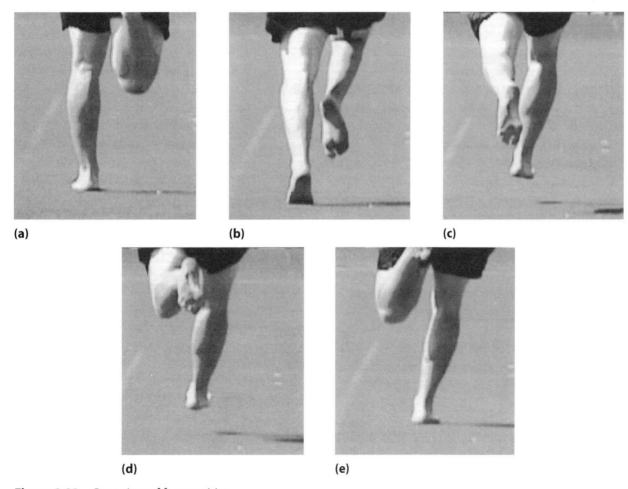

(a) (b) (c)

(d) (e)

Figure 3.23 Rear view of foot position

Figure 3.24 Foot is directly under head for good balance.

Figure 3.25 Swing leg is in front of thigh.

Because long-distance running is slower, but still comparatively fast in competition, (In the last marathon, the record runner ran an average 4-minute, 47-second mile! Most runners cannot duplicate this time for over a mile!) the leg is not brought back as forcefully and the landing is made slightly in front of the body. If you look from the side during the initial ground contact, the swing leg is still slightly behind by approximately 10 to 20 degrees. (See Fig. 3.26.)

For most fitness runners the exact separation between the thighs at the moment of foot contact is not critical. The key element here is that the forward leg is in front of the body and moves backward prior to contact. This not only decreases the amount of braking forces, but increases your stride length and makes running faster, more economical, and safer.

An effective way to learn the feel of the forward thigh drive is to concentrate on driving the knee forward. Check to see if the knee comes well in front of the body. It is important to get the feel of bringing the thigh forward rather than upward. In addition, you should experience landing on the ball-heel or middle of the foot and, as the thigh stops in front of the body, let the shin swing out.

To develop the pawback action, extend forward with the foot when swinging the shin forward after

the thigh is close to 40 or 50 degrees horizontal. Do not lead with the foot in the forward thigh drive since it is the thigh that is driven forward while the shin remains folded underneath the thigh. As the shin swings out it prepares the hamstring muscles

Figure 3.26 In long-distance running, the swing leg is slightly behind the thigh when ground contact is made.

to then pull an almost straight leg down and back to contact the ground.

The hands and fingers should remain relaxed at all times. The wrist should be relaxed, loose, and held basically in the neutral position. In sprinting it is possible to see the hand literally "flapping" during the run, which is indicative of high levels of relaxation. (See Fig. 3.27.) Seeing a fist or locked fingers indicates tension.

The position of your head governs your body position and balance. Be sure you have good posture with your head directly above your shoulders. The shoulders should be directly above the hips, which are directly above the feet in the support phase. If your head is forward you will find yourself leaning forward excessively, which requires even more energy to maintain balance.

A common sign of tension is facial strain. To determine if you are tense when running, smile every so often. If you feel a distinct change in your features (or in your body), then you know you have tension. The more relaxed the non-running muscles are, the more effective your running technique becomes and the less the energy you use. But if you are too relaxed you will not be able to run well; some tension is needed for good posture and effective muscle action.

Self Check

To see how well you execute the key elements of effective running, have someone videotape you. Be sure you are directly in line with the camera (side and front view) and that there is little panning. By keeping your body perpendicular to the camera you will get an accurate view of your actions when you view the videotape frame by frame. Compare yourself to some of the recommendations and photos presented in this book to see if there are any major differences, and then make the changes accordingly.

It is important that you run in your regular stride to get an accurate assessment. Having someone analyze you when you run at a different speed will be of little value. Also, if you have someone analyze your technique, be sure the individual is qualified. Being a running coach or sports doctor does not mean the individual is qualified to analyze. This is a highly specific skill.

(a)

(b)

Figure 3.27 Hand flapping indicates relaxation.

(a) (b) (c)

(d) (e)

Figure 3.28 This runner has a good pushoff, stride length, and posture, but he drops the swing-leg thigh too early as the shin swings out to make premature contact with the ground. In addition, his recovery leg is too high.

Figure 3.29 This is an outstanding marathon runner, but even here we see the leg is too straight on pushoff, too high on recovery, and the shoulder has slightly more rotation than desired.

(a)　　　　　　　(b)　　　　　　　(c)　　　　　　　(d)

(e)　　　　　　　(f)　　　　　　　(g)　　　　　　　(h)

Figure 3.30 Notice the erect running position, relaxed hands and body, strong pushoff, and powerful knee drive and pawback that this runner displays.

(i)　　　　(j)　　　　(k)　　　　(l)

(m)　　　　(n)

Figure 3.30　(continued)

(a) (b) (c) (d)

(e) (f) (g) (h)

(i) (j) (k) (l)

Figure 3.31 An early drop of the swing-leg thigh makes premature contact with the ground, and the pushoff leg is too straight. The shin carry and posture are this runner's strong points.

(m) (n) (o) (p)

(q) (r) (s) (t)

(u)

Figure 3.31 (continued)

(a) (b) (c) (d)

(e) (f) (g) (h)

Figure 3.32 Basically, good sprint technique is shown here. The leg recovery is slightly high, the support leg is excessively bent during support, and the arm action is too high and through too great a range of motion.

(i)   (j)   (k)   (l)

(m)   (n)   (o)   (p)

Figure 3.32   (continued)

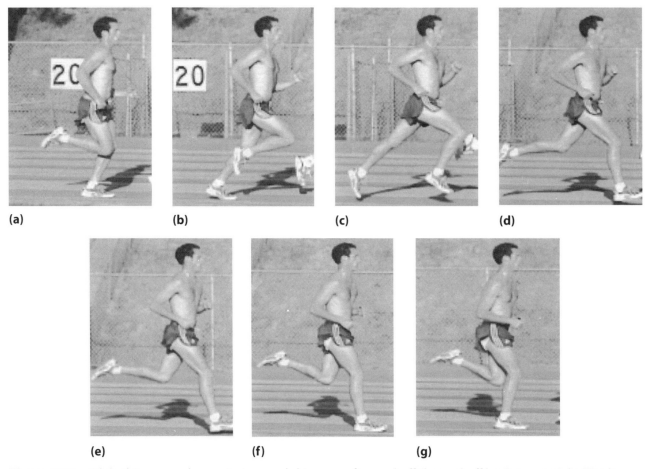

Figure 3.33 While this runner demonstrates good shin carry after pushoff, the pushoff leg is too straight. He also drops the swing-leg thigh too early.

Figure 3.34 This is a good example of sprint technique, showing powerful pawback, powerful arm drive and extension, and good pushoff and ankle action.

(e) **(f)** **(g)** **(h)**

(i) **(j)** **(k)** **(l)**

(m) **(n)** **(o)** **(p)**

(q)

Figure 3.34 (continued)

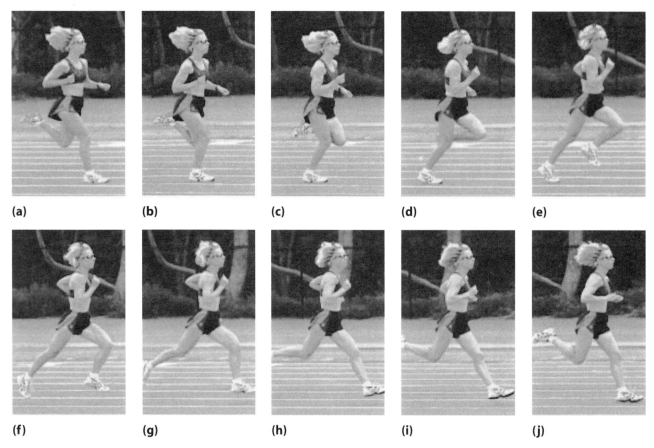

(a)　　　(b)　　　(c)　　　(d)　　　(e)

(f)　　　(g)　　　(h)　　　(i)　　　(j)

Figure 3.35　She displays good long-distance running technique except that the leg recovery is slightly too high, and she keeps too tight an angle in the elbow throughout the run. This indicates some tightness in the upper body.

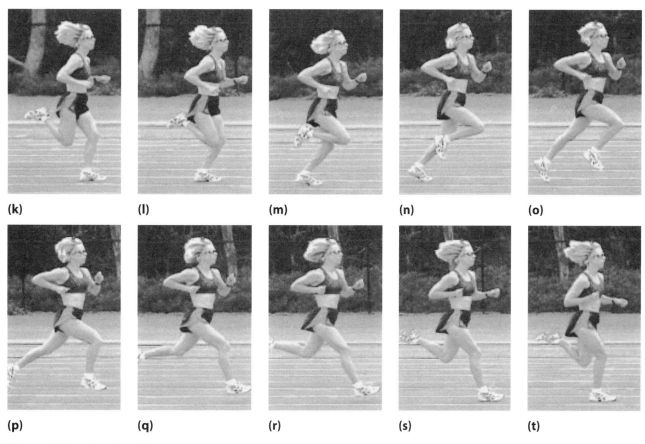

(k)   (l)   (m)   (n)   (o)

(p)   (q)   (r)   (s)   (t)

Figure 3.35   (continued)

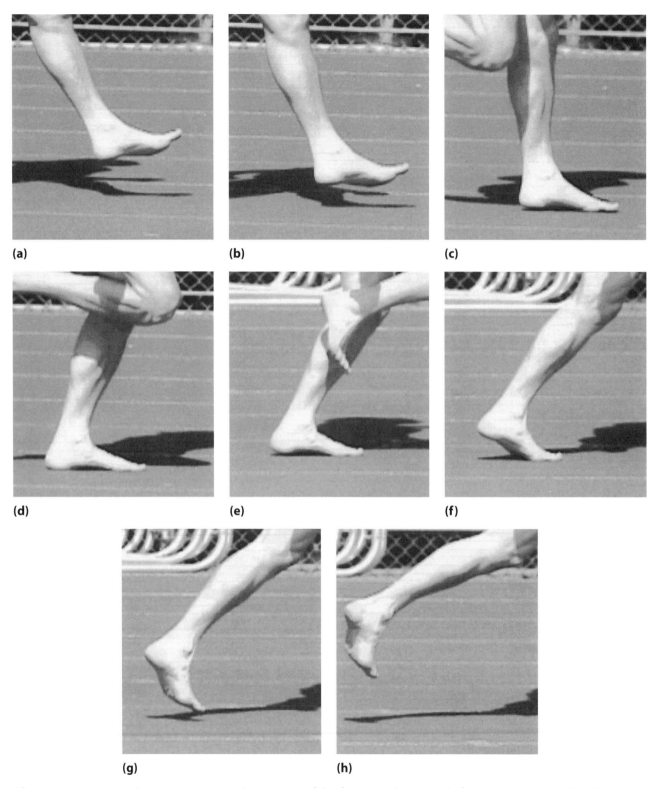

(a)　　　　　　　(b)　　　　　　　(c)

(d)　　　　　　　(e)　　　　　　　(f)

(g)　　　　　　　(h)

Figure 3.36　Notice the compression and expansion of the foot arch during and after contact. Also notice the muscular contractions during support, which indicate involvement of the muscle and tendons.

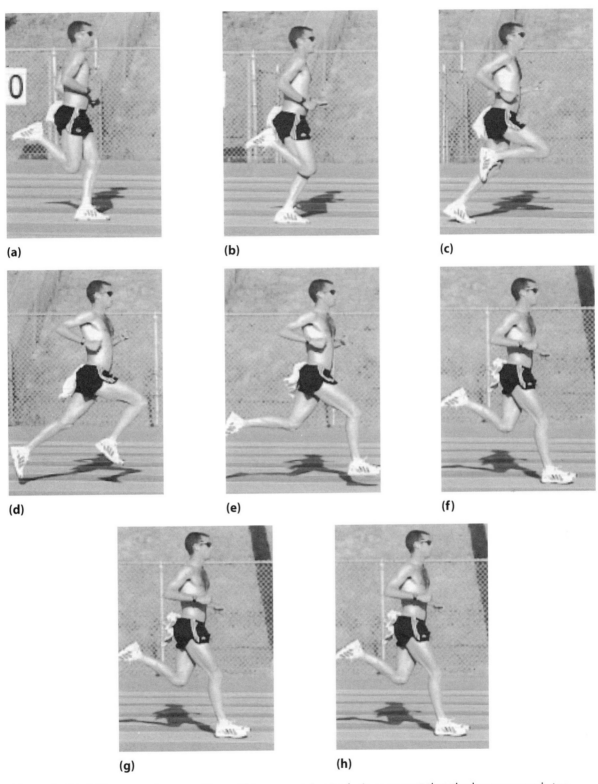

Figure 3.37 This runner has good long-distance running technique except that the leg recovery is too high and he lowers his swing leg too soon, cutting down on stride length and the ability to generate greater force from pawback.

Figure 3.38 The front view shows good forward knee drive but excessive shoulder rotation. Arms are moving sideways rather than forward and backward. She also shows excessive lean to the left side during the run.

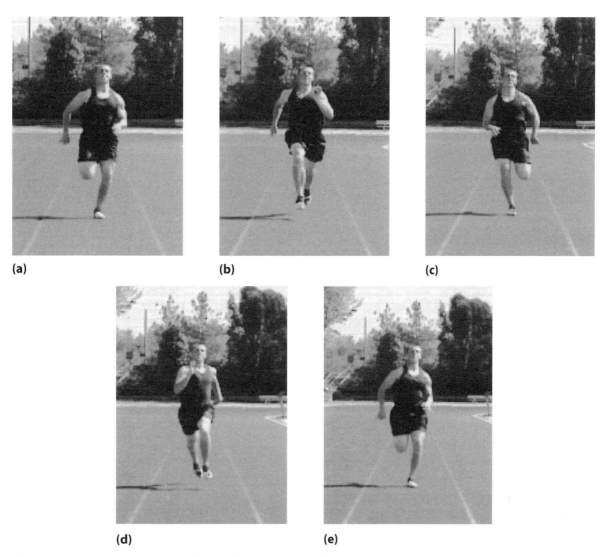

(a)   **(b)**   **(c)**

(d)   **(e)**

Figure 3.39   Here we see good forward knee drive and forward and backward arm action. Notice the leg's bowed position.

(a) (b) (c) (d)

(e) (f) (g) (h)

(i) (j) (k) (l)

Figure 3.40 Even though this is a high-level marathoner, his recovery leg is much too high and his pushoff leg is too straight. He is using more knee extension as opposed to ankle extension. You can see the vertical component in the pushoff by looking at the head in line with the fence.

(m)   (n)   (o)   (p)

(q)   (r)   (s)   (t)

(u)   (v)   (w)   (x)

Figure 3.40   (continued)

(a)   (b)   (c)

(d)   (e)   (f)

(g)   (h)

Figure 3.41   This runner shows basically good running technique except for an early letdown of the swing leg to make premature contact with the ground. Also, leg recovery is slightly too high.

Kinesiology of Running

Running speed stems mainly from three joint actions: ankle-joint extension (pushoff), hip-joint flexion (knee drive), and hip-joint extension (pawback). Other actions can also play significant roles but their importance depends on the running speed. These include shoulder-joint flexion (arm drive), arm and shoulder-joint extension (straightening and simultaneously driving the arm down), a 90-degree elbow angle and lateral hip rotation (in long-distance running), transverse (forward and back) pelvic-girdle rotation, shoulder rotation, and ankle dorsi flexion (raising the foot while whipping the shin forward). When these actions are optimized, you may get additional speed and economy, which can improve your performance.

In this chapter, each joint action is described in relation to the muscles involved and how they are integrated. This will give you a better understanding of how muscles function to produce speed and economy, and how failing to correctly integrate the muscles can cause injury. Knowledge of the muscles and how they work is also needed to create the specific exercises you need to strengthen weaker muscles and enhance stronger muscles.

(For greater clarity, each body action is dealt with separately. However, some of these actions occur simultaneously and overlap one another in the sequence of movements.)

Role and Action of Muscles and Tendons

To better understand how muscles and tendons function during the running stride, it is necessary to understand some of their basic physiological functions. The muscles of the body occur in pairs. One set of muscles on one side of a joint executes a movement and another set of muscles on the opposite side of the joint executes the opposite movement. The muscles involved in executing a particular movement are known as the agonists, and the opposing muscles are known as the antagonists.

The agonists and antagonists have a very close relationship to one another and are involved in all movements. When one set of muscles contracts concentrically (shortens) to produce a movement, the muscles on the opposite side of the joint contract eccentrically (lengthen). In this lengthening, or stretching, the muscles become more tensed as the range of motion increases and when the tension becomes great enough, the movement stops. The eccentric contraction plays a very important role in running by controlling movements, stopping movements, and preparing the muscles for powerful and explosive contractions.

The muscles can switch from one type of contraction to another depending on the movement being done, the intensity of the stimulation, and the forces encountered. When muscles contract but the force is not great enough to produce movement, it is known as a static, or isometric, contraction. The muscles are tensed in an attempt to create movement, but because external resistance is so great, they cannot overcome it and no movement ensues.

The knee drive can be used as an example to illustrate the different muscle contractions. In this action, the hip-flexor muscles contract concentrically to drive the thigh forward. As the leg is driven forward, the hamstrings contract eccentrically to control the movement and range of motion. As these muscles stretch, the tension builds up until it is great enough to stop the forward movement. At the moment the forward movement stops, the hamstrings contract isometrically and then the contraction switches to the concentric as the leg is driven down and back. As this action takes place, the hip flexors contract eccentrically.

When there is great loading of the muscles, as occurs on touchdown, the foot, ankle, knee, and hip joints undergo flexion, which is controlled by the eccentric contraction of the extensor muscles of these joints. The greater the load (landing forces), the stronger the eccentric contraction needed to stop the downward movement of the body. If the eccentric contraction is not sufficiently strong, excessive flexion in the joints will create too much down movement of the body.

The eccentric contraction is also the most important contraction for developing the tension needed in the muscle to execute an explosive muscular contraction. If you purposely contract a muscle, it takes up to 0.8 seconds before the muscle achieves maximum tension. If it took that long during running,

you would not be able to run fast. Most muscular contractions in sprint running occur in less than 0.10 seconds. For example, the foot is in contact with the ground for 0.10 seconds or less. Half of this time is for the landing and half for takeoff. In 0.05 seconds the muscle develops sufficient tension to stop the downward movement. In addition, accumulating enough energy in the eccentric contraction allows the muscles to contract explosively in the concentric contraction in order to execute the pushoff.

The tendons stretch and return to their initial length in a manner similar to the muscles because of their elasticity. When they are forcefully stretched, they return to their initial shape quickly and forcefully due to their resiliency. They work in conjunction with the muscles in a way that conserves muscular energy.

Foot Actions

When you land on the ball of the foot or mid-foot, the muscles and tendons of the foot arch are the first to come into play. They undergo a quick forceful stretch and gain tension for initial shock absorption. They then undergo even greater tension and, as a result, accumulate energy, which is then given back in the pushoff. This is a very important role of the foot!

Because of this it is surprising that strength exercises for the foot are rarely recommended for runners. This may be due to the belief that running shoes can duplicate or enhance the functions of the foot. In reality, the shoes do not come close to doing this, and in many cases they actually interfere with the proper functioning of the foot and leg muscles and tendons. According to some researchers running shoes *lead to* foot, ankle, knee, and hip problems instead of preventing them. They have even found that the number of running injuries increases with the price of the shoes! Rather than relying on running shoes, you should strengthen the foot muscles, tendons, and ligaments so the feet and legs can perform their normal functions more effectively than any shoe. And, you should wear shoes that allow your feet to function normally.

The Knee Drive

The forward drive of the swing-leg thigh, which involves the hip-joint flexor muscles, begins in the flight phase and is later synchronized with ankle-joint extension. The muscles, including the iliopsoas (iliacus and psoas), pectineus, and the rectus femoris of the quadriceps, go into action soon after pushoff when the leg is behind the body and the pelvis is rotated forward. In this position, the lower-abdominal and hip-flexor muscles are tensed from the eccentric contraction that occurred as the upper body moved forward during the support phase and as the pushoff leg moved backward.

The hip-flexor muscles together with the lower abdominals contract explosively in the concentric contraction so the thigh can accelerate forward. The thigh then moves forward on momentum. As the thigh approaches its forwardmost position, it stops and the shin swings out to fully extend the leg. The thigh stops when the hamstrings develop sufficient eccentric tension. The tension becomes even greater as the shin swings out and the leg straightens to initiate the pawback action (pulling the leg back and down for touchdown).

The Pushoff

The calf muscles are the key muscles involved in the pushoff, which basically consists of ankle-joint extension. If you use the quadriceps to fully extend the leg at the knee joint in the pushoff, you will no longer be running, you will be leaping! Thus, during the pushoff, a slightly bent knee remains firmly in position as the ankle extension takes place. For this the quadriceps undergoes an isometric contraction to hold the leg position.

Of the two calf muscles involved in ankle extension, the gastrocnemius is most important in sprints, while the soleus is most important in endurance running. In general, the soleus has more red, slow-twitch fibers, which are considered endurance fibers since they have great lasting power. The gastrocnemius consists of more white, fast-twitch fibers, which contribute to quick, explosive contractions that are more suitable to sprinting. However, these muscles can be trained to act more as explosive or endurance fibers.

In addition to the calf muscles, the Achilles tendon is also strongly involved in the pushoff. In some runners, especially those who have very effective running technique, the Achilles tendon may play a greater role than the calf muscles in relation to producing the pushoff force. Studies have shown that the Achilles tendon can return 60 to 70 percent of the energy generated in the landing—substantially more than the muscles can generate by themselves.

Pawback (Pullback)

After the swing-leg thigh is driven forward, the leg is extended and then brought back forcefully to make contact with the ground via contraction of the hamstrings and the gluteus maximus. The greater the speed with which the leg is brought down and back, the greater the force generated on touchdown. This in turn creates greater tension (loading) of the leg muscles, which can then be used in the pushoff. In addition, the faster the leg is brought back, the more the landing is on the ball of the foot to tense the foot and Achilles tendon.

When you land first on the ball of the foot and then on the heel, or on mid-foot, the Achilles tendon is immediately activated. Its role is to somewhat cushion the landing (in addition to the work of the foot-arch muscles and tendons) but mainly to withstand and accumulate the landing forces (store energy) for giveback in the pushoff.

The hamstring and gluteus maximus play the key roles in the pawback. They become strongly pretensed in the eccentric contraction as they stop the forward movement of the thigh. As the lower leg swings out, the muscles stretch even more and the tension increases greatly to stop forward leg movement and to quickly and forcefully pull the leg back and down.

When the foot is in full contact with the ground, the hamstring and buttock muscles relax somewhat to allow for hip flexion. The knee-joint flexion, which is controlled by the eccentric contraction of the quadriceps, plays the major role in support and assists in cushioning the landing. The hip-joint extensor muscles are not involved in the pushoff. When the leg moves behind the body, it may appear as though these muscles are actively involved, but it is forward pelvic-girdle rotation via concentric contraction of the lower-back muscles.

Shoulder Flexion (Forward Arm Drive)

The forward arm action uses mainly the anterior deltoid and upper pectoralis—major muscles of the shoulder joint. The forward action begins explosively when the elbow is up and behind the body and then slows down and stops as the arm comes close to the vertical position alongside the body. The forward motion is stopped by the eccentric contraction of the posterior deltoid, the long head of the triceps, latissimus dorsi, and teres major.

The arm action mimics the hip-joint action in relation to range of motion. If you have sufficient flexibility in the shoulder joint and your arm goes through the necessary range of motion, the thigh in the knee drive will go through its full range (when you have the necessary hip-joint flexibility) for greater efficiency. Thus it is important that the arm and leg actions are synchronized and that you have the needed strength and flexibility to achieve the needed range of motion.

Shoulder-Joint Extension

In sprinting, shoulder-joint extension is extremely powerful, especially when coupled with elbow extension (arm straightening). These actions are used to forcefully bring the arm down and back in order to place a greater load on the leg muscles. The shoulder action involves the posterior deltoid and the long head of the triceps. In the initial movement, the latissimus dorsi and the teres major are also involved. In long-distance running, however, since the elbow remains bent at 90 degrees, the shoulder-extension action is not strong. The mus-

cles involved in shoulder-joint extension also bring the elbow up and back behind the body in preparation for the forward drive of the arm.

Arm Extension

Arm (elbow-joint) extension occurs mainly in sprints and involves the triceps in a concentric contraction. The long head of the triceps tenses eccentrically to stop the forward arm drive, and the two other heads of the triceps are tensed when the elbow is flexed during the forward arm drive. All three heads then contract strongly to straighten the arm as it is whipped down toward the ground to create greater pushoff force. After this action, the long head of the triceps and the posterior deltoid raise the arm (elbow) up behind the body to prepare for the forward arm drive.

Static Elbow-Joint Flexion

Static elbow-joint flexion is used mainly in long-distance running. In sprinting, the arm straightens during the back movement phase; passively bends in the elbow as it is raised to the rear; and then drives forward, bending to a 90-degree angle. Developing the muscles involved in bending the elbow (elbow flexion) can assist in both sprinting and long-distance running. The major muscles involved in elbow flexion and in holding the 90-degree angle are the biceps and brachialis.

Shoulder Rotation

Some shoulder rotation occurs in almost all runners, but this is not a desired action since it does not contribute to speed or running economy. In fact, the more shoulder rotation you have, the poorer your running form and the less speed you can generate. Minimizing shoulder rotation is a key role of the forward and backward arm action. When the shoulders are square to the running direction, the arm action holds them in that position. However, if you swing the arms at an angle, the shoulders will have a greater tendency to rotate.

The trunk muscles responsible for holding the shoulders in place are mainly the internal and external obliques of the abdomen and the erector spinae muscles of the lower back. When these muscles are strong, they stabilize the shoulders and pelvic girdle. Lower-back muscle strength should be sufficiently strong to balance the strength of the abdominal obliques. You should never keep the abdominals contracted when running; they should work only when needed. Consciously contracting the abdominals leads to greater fatigue and a bent-over posture that interferes with the forward leg drive.

Hip Rotation

The muscles of the hip joint (abductors, adductors, flexors, and extensors) play a very important role in stabilizing the pelvis during the dynamic leg actions. The key abductors are located on the outer sides of the hips and hold the pelvis level, providing lateral stability to the hips and outside knee. These muscles, together with the hip medial and lateral rotators, prevent horizontal hip rotation, and keep the pelvis stable to allow for powerful contractions of the hip-flexor and extensor muscles. In addition, the abductors play a very important role in limiting lateral pelvic-girdle rotation. These muscles hold the hips level so there are no unwanted up and down side rotational movements of the pelvis, which are uneconomical and detract from effective forward and backward movements of the thigh. (These muscles are most important in race walking.)

The adductors, located on the inner thigh, are involved in initiating the forward knee drive and not allowing the thigh to drift outward. These muscles are relatively big and strong.

Many athletes and coaches erroneously believe the pelvis rotates sideways in a forward direction with each stride in order to increase stride length. It is, of course, possible to increase stride length by this method, but it is costly. For example, if the pelvis rotates to the left to allow the right leg to move far-

ther forward, the right leg, instead of being planted in a straight line directly in front of the body midline, will most likely be planted to the left of the body midline. You end up running in a zigzag fashion rather than in a straight line. In sprinting, when the pelvis remains basically stable, you could draw a straight line between each foot plant. Thus the hip muscles, in addition to playing a major role in the production of running speed, also play a very important role in stabilizing the pelvis. A stable pelvis stabilizes the shoulders and eliminates unwanted rotational actions. This makes running more effective and economical.

Shoulder Elevation

The upper-trapezius muscle and the levator scapulae play an important role in maintaining the shoulders in their normal upright position. This is needed to ensure effective arm actions and to maintain good upper-body posture. If these muscles are weak there is a tendency to drop the shoulders and become round-shouldered. As a result, the arms cross the body and the arm drive loses its effectiveness.

Back Extension

Back extension, or more accurately, maintaining an erect trunk position, is very important in effective running. When you have an erect trunk, it allows for effective thigh actions, which are the key to increasing running speed. Leaning forward occurs only when accelerating; when you are in full stride you must have an erect position. A few degrees of forward lean are acceptable in sprinting, but it is best to be fully erect in long-distance running.

The ability to hold the trunk erect depends on the strength of the lower-back muscles and hip-flexor muscle flexibility. If these flexor muscles are tight, they tilt the pelvis forward, which in turn pulls the upper body forward, creating excessive forward lean. This positioning prevents lower-back muscles from playing their key role of keeping you erect and leads to premature touchdown.

5

Active Stretches for Runners

Static stretches have become well accepted in the United States and are practiced by most runners. For anyone to suggest that runners should not do such stretches is almost sacrilegious. But if we closely examine the research done on static stretches in running and other sports as well as practical experiences, we will see that static stretches do not truly prepare you for running or prevent injury.

In static stretches you hold a particular position for up to thirty or more seconds to stretch the muscles and connective tissue surrounding the joint being worked. For example, it is not uncommon to see runners leaning into a wall to stretch the Achilles tendon and calf muscles for fairly long periods of time or bending over to touch the toes to stretch the hamstrings. The key to successful execution of these stretches is to hold the position while relaxing the muscles as much as possible to get a gradual increase in the range of motion. These static stretches require muscle relaxation, which is needed to counteract the muscle, and tendon reflexes, which tend to hold back any increases in range of motion.

Running is a very dynamic sport that requires active and often forceful movements of the legs and arms, especially in sprinting. The joint actions in running are ballistic in nature, i.e., they are initiated with a strong muscular contraction to accelerate the limb and place it in motion, after which it continues on its own momentum. The movement is stopped by contraction of the antagonist muscles. Such ballistic movements create great forces that the body must deal with to absorb and accumulate energy for giveback in the pushoff action.

When you do static stretching, the amount of force exerted is insignificant. More important, during the static stretch the muscles are completely relaxed, whereas in running the muscles perform dynamically in both concentric and eccentric contractions. The forces experienced in such movements far surpass those experienced in static stretching. As a result, you can never prepare yourself adequately to cope with forceful movements if you do only static stretches. This is one reason it is not uncommon to find injuries occurring. Recent studies show that static stretches done prior to running do not decrease the number of injuries experienced by runners.

Even proprioceptive neuromuscular facilitation (PNF) stretches do not truly prepare the muscles. Here you hold a given static stretch for a few seconds and then release it before it becomes uncomfortable. After a very brief rest you stretch again trying to increase the range of motion of that joint a little more before again releasing it for a moment. Producing phases of intense muscular tension followed by reflexive relaxation of opposing muscle groups is still only a partial solution to the problem of producing functional natural flexibility. PNF stretches may do this only if they are specific to the movements experienced in running. In addition, they must be specific to the muscular recruitment pattern and speed of limb movements. Doing this requires a highly qualified specialist.

The range of motion seen in running at both slow and fast speeds is determined by how strongly the muscles contract to move the limbs. An active range of motion is determined by the strength of the muscles involved, not by the amount of flexibility you have. The muscular contraction creates the force needed to move the limb through the possible range of motion.

If you have a flexibility range of 180 degrees but the muscles are only strong enough to move the limb voluntarily through 150 degrees, the remaining 30 degrees of freedom will not be seen. Because of this, to truly prepare the muscles for running, stretches must take the muscles through the range of motion in which they must operate in the running stride. You must involve the muscles and the corresponding nerves that send signals to the muscles for a timely contraction with the correct intensity.

In static stretching the nervous system is literally knocked out so that it cannot activate the muscles to ensure adequate stretching. This is contradictory to what occurs in running. For example, in static stretching as you hold the stretch and the range of motion is increased, the antagonist muscles being stretched have a tendency to contract to limit the range of motion possible. Instead of allowing the muscles to contract you must voluntarily relax these muscles to eliminate the stretch reflex to allow for a greater range of motion. As a result, the nervous system does not play a major role in static stretching.

In running, however, the nervous system plays an extremely important role. Running is a neuromuscular activity since it requires constant firing of the nerves to activate the muscles to continually produce the leg and arm actions. This is a very active process. To truly prepare the muscles and joints for running you must do some activity to properly prepare the muscles and joints involved.

The main purpose of stretching is to elongate the tissues either temporarily or permanently. When a stretch is done it produces either elastic extension (lengthening of the involved tissues with a later return to normal), plastic deformation (in which the lengthening becomes permanent), or tissue rupture. Exactly what happens depends on the amount of force used and the duration of the force.

Since tissue tearing is not desirable, the stretch should produce either elastic extension or plastic deformation. When there is elastic extension, the stretching produces a temporary change or elongation. This is good when the subsequent running is of relatively short duration and takes place soon after the stretching session. But a short-term increase in range of motion has much more to do with nervous processes than stretching.

The main outcome of most static stretching is to permanently elongate the relevant tissues through plastic deformation. This is desirable if you have a limited range of motion due to a shortened length of some component of the muscle or ligament complex. If the range of motion is not limited, then static stretching may be ill-advised because increasing range of motion by static stretching may compromise joint integrity. Excessive stretching may stretch the ligaments or other tissues to such a degree that they no longer are elastic and do not return to their original shape and size. This may be a reason for the increased number of injuries that occurs in runners and other athletes—the excessive static stretching results in weaker joints that are more susceptible to injury. The problem is compounded even more if no supplementary strength training is done to maintain joint integrity.

Most effective is to stretch and strengthen the joint-support structures simultaneously through the same range of motion. Full-range exercises against resistance offer the greatest functional increase in range of motion. When the stretches are accompanied by strengthening, the danger of injury decreases tremendously, and more important, the muscles and joints are prepared for forthcoming activity.

Stretches that are active in nature truly warm up and prepare the muscles for action, which is an important goal of stretching in the warm-up. As the term implies, *warm-up* means to increase the temperature of the muscle prior to participation. By doing active stretches involving the muscles and joints through a full range of motion, you warm up the muscles and prepare them for the activity.

It is important to understand that stretching and flexibility training are not necessarily synonymous. Some flexibility exercises may increase range of motion but are not considered stretches because the modifications in the range of motion rely entirely on the neuromuscular processes, as with the muscle and tendon reflexes that control the functional range of movement. This is why you should differentiate between types of stretching and flexibility exercises in order to perform the most appropriate and effective static and dynamic means of increasing functional range of motion. Unfortunately, the value of stretching that has permeated the literature is related to increasing joint mobility rather than achieving functional range of motion in the shoulder, hip, knee, and ankle joints as they are involved in running.

Another way of looking at functional range of motion is to equate the stretch with exactly what takes place in the joint. Does the stretch duplicate what takes place in the joint in relation to the range of motion? Does the stretch duplicate the type of muscular contraction elicited during an action? For example, studies have shown that the landing forces in running çan often be three to ten times body weight, depending on running speed and how one lands. These are great forces that the muscles and joints must be able to handle. The joints and their associated tissues must be able to cope with expected *and* unexpected irregular and sudden loads, as when you are running on uneven surfaces.

If the tissues are unable to dampen shock loading adequately or with optimal speed, like efficient shock absorbers on a car, then the hard and soft tissues of the body may be damaged. However, if the tissues are too soft or too stiff then shock loading may also damage the body.

All too often stretch training elongates tissues while disregarding what is taking place in the joints. For example, in the standing toe touch done by many runners to stretch the hamstrings, you bend-over from the hips and waist in an attempt to touch the toes. You remain in the bent-over position for thirty to sixty seconds, but instead of fully stretching the hamstring muscles you end up stretching the lower-back ligaments.

The standing (and seated) toe-touch exercises produce a poor stretch of the hamstrings but are excellent stretches of the lower-back ligaments that hold the vertebrae in place. As a result of doing such stretches over a long period of time, you will have permanently stretched back ligaments that create a loosely held lumbar spine prone to injury. To understand the inadequacy of the standing straight-leg toe touch, do the following: Assume a standing position and lock the back in its normal curvature. There should be slight arching in the lumbar spine. Hold the spine in place by contracting the lower-back muscles and then bend over from the hips, not from the waist. As you bend over, the hips must move to the rear as the trunk inclines forward. Based on my experience working with runners, I feel confident that most of you will not get beyond a 45-degree forward lean.

Look to see where your hands are when your trunk is inclined forward while still holding the normal curvature of the spine. For most of you the hands may be approximately knee high or higher. If you are capable of touching your toes when the back is rounded, it means the length of your lower legs is the distance over which you stretched the lower back, not the hamstrings. If you instead hold a bent-over-from-the-hips position with normal lumbar spinal curvature (slight arch) for several seconds, you will feel a much stronger stretch of the hamstring muscles.

It should also be noted that bending over from the hips is a very safe way of bending over when trying to pick up or reach something. Avoid the rounded-back position as much as possible since it can be a major culprit in lower-back problems.

Runners and other athletes often think of stretching, or, more accurately, flexibility training, as separate from other forms of training, especially strength training. This is a major error. Flexibility training should assume the same importance as strength and other types of training and should be integrated into the total training regime. Stretches should not be done only before running or some other activity. If you truly require additional flexibility, then flexibility training should be an important part of your total training and the flexibility training should be coupled with strength training.

Active stretches stretch the muscles and prepare them for activity. When you do active stretches with resistance you can gain strength through the full range of motion in which you do the flexibility exercise. In other words, it is possible to gain strength and flexibility simultaneously in the same exercise. This cuts down on the amount of time needed for such training and you get a greater benefit. When active stretches are done, the newly created range of motion is functional, which means it will be involved in your running. It is a useable range of motion in which the muscles are capable of moving the limb through the range of motion developed.

We live in an age of sports specialization. Running is not merely the simple act of going out and moving one leg in front of the other in a cyclical fashion. It is a learned skill that can be made more effective and efficient. Your performance can be improved greatly with proper training in relation to how you run and exercises that are specific to running, including the active stretches that duplicate what occurs in running.

There are many forms of active stretches that range from relatively simple stretches to very complex, explosive stretches. However, in all cases active stretches involve muscular work during the stretch to ensure maximum joint safety and prepare the muscles for a forthcoming action. In addition, active stretches can involve contracting muscles to perform a movement that stretches the antagonist muscles. It is also possible to do active stretches with gravity providing the force to go through the range of motion.

The major muscular contraction involved in active stretches is the eccentric contraction. In this contraction the muscle develops tension but the overall length of the muscle increases, or stretches, under tension. For example, in running, when you experience touchdown there is slight flexion in the ankle, knee, and hip joints to absorb and withstand some of the landing forces. As soon as the foot touches the ground, and in many cases prior to touchdown, the muscles and tendons immediately tense to handle the forces and accumulate energy.

When flexion takes place in the ankle, knee, and hip joints, the muscles lengthen and tense to control the flexion (down movement). But as the muscles lengthen they develop more and more tension. Once the muscle tension becomes great enough it stops the movement and you remain in a stable position. When you push off, the muscles shorten, or contract, concentrically. Thus the muscles work in unison. When the agonist muscles perform the action, the antagonist muscles limit and stop the action and at the same time prepare the muscles for what is usually the next action to be performed.

Instead of thinking only in terms of the muscles that need stretching, in order to make the stretch specific to what occurs in running, you should think in terms of muscle and joint actions. Doing this will give you a better understanding of how stretches relate to the key actions that occur and how they not only prepare you for running, but improve your running.

Ankle Extension (and Foot Flexion)

Touchdown and pushoff are controlled by the muscles and support structures of the foot, mainly the arch, and lower leg, mainly the Achilles tendon and the gastrocnemius and soleus muscles of the calf. The gastrocnemius is especially important as you increase running speed. The soleus is active at all speeds but especially in slow, prolonged running.

On a mid-foot touchdown, in which ankle-joint flexion takes place, it is important to have strength and flexibility of the gastrocnemius, Achilles tendon, and support structure of the foot arch. In takeoff, foot extension (plantar flexion) takes place, which is determined by the calf muscles and tendons and by the range of motion possible in extension. The best stretches to improve the range of motion in this action are standing ankle extensions.

1. Wall Stretch. Stand with your feet flat on the ground two to four feet away from a wall or fence and place your hands against the wall, approximately shoulder high. Stand far enough away from the wall to feel the stretch. As you lower your heels to contact the ground (or lean into the wall) you should feel a strong eccentric stretch of the tendons and muscles. Hold the position for about one to two seconds, then rise up on the balls of your feet, holding the up position for two seconds. Lower your heels at a moderate rate of speed until you feel the stretch, hold momentarily, then again rise up on the balls of the feet and hold. The holding on top is important for concentration on full ankle-joint extension during pushoff. (See Fig. 5.1.) This stretch can also be done on a stair step by holding the railing for support. Also execute on one or both feet simultaneously.

2. Seated Ankle-Joint Extension. This stretch is mainly for increased range of motion. Assume a seated position on your lower legs, ground contact on knees and instep of the feet with buttocks on heels. Place your hands alongside or in front of your knees and shift most of your weight onto your hands. When you are ready, sit back so your buttocks are over your heels and apply downward pressure to the ankle joint. Sit back for two to three seconds, then shift the weight back onto your hands to relieve the pressure on the feet, and then push down with the feet to raise your hips. The range of motion is not great. The key to doing this stretch is to be able to achieve greater extension in the ankle joint, which then allows you to get a full range of motion in the pushoff. (See Fig. 5.2.) The seated ankle-joint extension exercise also stretches and strengthens the

(a) **(b)**

Figure 5.1   Wall stretch

(a) **(b)**

Figure 5.2   Seated ankle-joint extension

tibialis anterior muscle in the front of the shin. It is responsible for flexing the foot when whipping the shin forward, after the knee drive.

Leg (Knee) Flexion and Extension

A great range-of-flexion or extension motion in the knee joint is not necessary for runners since it is never seen in the running stride. The knee joint undergoes flexion (eccentric stretch) on landing but less bending means more effective running. Achieving a 45-degree angle in the knee joint is usually more than sufficient to stretch the muscles involved and prepare them for the support phase in running.

3. Squat Stretch. To do the squat, which stretches the quadriceps, stand with your feet hip-width apart, feet flat on the ground, and trunk erect. Lock the lower back in its normal curvature (slightly arched lumbar spine) and then slowly go into a squat. As you bend your knees your hips should move slightly to the rear and your trunk should incline forward while the spine remains stable. Lower the body (think of lowering the hips) while keeping the normal curvature of the spine at all times. Stop before the thigh-parallel position or

when there is a 45- to 90-degree angle between the back of the thigh and shin. Rise up, relax, and then repeat. Be sure the heels stay in contact with the ground, which in turn provides an Achilles stretch and ensures that the knees stay over the feet to prevent knee injury as you lower the body. (See Fig. 5.3.)

Note: The common static quadriceps stretch, also known as the butt-kick stretch, is potentially dangerous. In this stretch, the thigh is held vertical (perpendicular to the ground) and you pull the lower leg in to bring the heel of the foot close to the buttocks. This is a potentially dangerous position as you are pulling the knee joint apart. Since this position is never assumed in the running stride, this stretch is unnecessary. When the heel comes close to the buttocks in sprinting, the knee is forward of the body, which gives the quadriceps more slack and no additional stretching is needed.

Hip Flexion and Extension

Hip flexion and extension play key roles in determining running speed. They control stride length, effectiveness of the pushoff, and running speed. Thus it is important to have ample flexibility in the hip joints. Hip-flexor flexibility is most important

(a)

(b)

Figure 5.3 Squat stretch

in determining stride length. Hip-extensor (hamstring) flexibility determines how high the thigh can be raised before the leg straightens prior to the pullback. The greater your hip-flexor muscle flexibility, the greater the separation of the thighs in the pushoff and the faster your running speed.

Hip Flexion

The hip-joint flexor and adductor muscles are involved in hip flexion. The adductors initiate hip flexion and then allow the stronger hip flexors to take over when they are in better position. Do the lunge to stretch the hip flexors, and the side lunge, also known as the groin stretch, to isolate the hip-joint adductor muscles.

4. Lunge (Hip-Flexor Stretch). Assume a standing position with your feet hip-width apart. Take a very long step with one leg and plant your foot with the toes facing forward. Keep your trunk erect and slowly lower your body (eccentric stretch). Keep the rear leg straight but relaxed with your weight supported on the front leg. Before long you will feel a strong stretch of the hip flexors. Hold the down position for one to two seconds and then push off with the forward leg to assume the initial standing position. Repeat with the opposite leg. Be sure to keep your torso erect and the rear leg straight but relaxed as you do the exercise. If you lean forward or bend the rear leg you will not get an effective stretch of the hip-flexor muscles. (See Fig. 5.4.)

5. Side Lunge. Assume a standing position with your feet shoulder-width apart, arms alongside your body. Step directly out to the side and plant your foot at a 45-degree angle to the outside. Keep your torso erect and slowly lower your body so your weight is concentrated on the forward leg, while keeping the rear (pushoff) leg straight. In this position you will feel the groin stretch almost immediately. Hold the bottom position for one to two seconds and then rise up and repeat with the other leg. (See Fig. 5.5.)

Hip Extension

The hip extensors must be actively stretched to prepare them for pulling the leg back and down to make contact with the ground and to propel the body forward. These muscles also play a role in relation to how far the swing-leg thigh can be driven forward during the pushoff without adversely rotating the hips. The hip extensors (the gluteus maximus and hamstring muscles) can be stretched with or without active participation of the hip flexors.

(a)

(b)

Figure 5.4 Lunge

(a)

(b)

Figure 5.5   Side lunge

6. Lying Leg Raise.   To do the stretch with active involvement of the hip flexors, lie on your back with your arms alongside your body and legs out straight. When you are ready, hold one leg straight and raise it up as high as possible (but not past the vertical position). Then lower to the floor and raise up again in a continuous action. When the leg is raised via the concentric contraction of the hip flexors, the hip extensors undergo an eccentric stretch. With every leg raise you should be able to go a little further in your range of motion. After doing the stretch with one leg, repeat with the other leg. You can also alternate the legs during execution. (See Fig. 5.6.)

7. The Good Morning.   This active stretch does not involve the hip flexors and uses gravity as the moving force. The good morning exercise isolates the action to the hamstrings. (The gluteus maximus is also involved if you go through a sufficient range of motion.) To execute this stretch, assume a standing position with your feet hip-width apart. When ready, contract the lower-back muscles to lock the lumbar spine in its normal, slightly arched curvature. Hold your spine in position and legs straight and then bend forward from the hips until you feel a strong stretch of the hamstrings. Push the hips back as you bend forward.

(a)

(b)

Figure 5.6   Lying leg raise

(a)

(b)

Figure 5.7 The good morning

For most runners, the incline will be approximately 30 to 45 degrees forward. Be sure to maintain the normal curvature of the spine as you feel the eccentric stretch of the hamstring muscles and tendons. Hold for one to two seconds. Rise up by contracting the hamstrings concentrically and then relax before repeating. Every time you bend over, try to go through a slightly greater range of motion. (See Fig. 5.7.)

Forward and Backward Hip Rotation

Because of the structure of the hip joints, it is impossible to bring the leg forward and backward as occurs in the full running stride, especially in sprinting, without also involving anterior and posterior pelvis rotation. The axis for hip rotation is in the waist so that the upper part of the pelvis moves through the greatest range of motion. This requires ample midsection flexibility and strength to ensure a full range of motion.

8. Anterior Pelvic-Girdle Rotation. Assume a standing position with your torso erect and feet hip-width apart. When you are ready, contract the lower-back muscles (arch the back) and push the upper pelvis forward. Relax your upper body and allow the abdominal wall to relax so that the pelvis pushes the abdominal wall forward while your head and shoulders remain in place. Hold the forward position for one to two seconds and then return to the initial position and relax. Repeat when you are ready. (See Fig. 5.8.)

9. Posterior Pelvic-Girdle Rotation. Assume a standing position with your feet hip-width apart and your torso erect but relaxed. When ready, contract your abdominal muscles and then flatten and round the lower back as much as possible. Do this by pushing the top of the pelvis to the rear. Hold the abdominal contraction for one to two seconds. Relax and return to the initial position. Repeat when you are ready. (See Fig. 5.9.)

Arm Flexion and Arm Extension

The range of motion in the shoulder is very important in increasing stride length. You need as much flexibility in the shoulder joint as you do in the hip joint to ensure a full range of motion in both joints so that the leg and arm movements can be synchronized.

(a)

(b)

Figure 5.8 Anterior pelvic-girdle rotation

(a)

(b)

Figure 5.9 Posterior pelvic-girdle rotation

Arm Flexion

For most runners there is usually ample flexibility in the shoulder joint to allow full range in arm flexion (the forward arm drive). The key is to be able to raise the elbows sufficiently high behind the body to a point where arm flexion begins. Thus, most of the stretching is to see how far you can bring the arm (elbow) backward and upward to ensure a full range of motion for the forward arm action. Two of the best exercises to do this are arm flexion from a lying-back position and the bent-arm elbow raise.

10. Arm Flexion from a Lying-Back Position. Assume a lying-back position on an exercise bench with your arm(s) hanging down as low as possible (you should

feel a stretch in the shoulder joints). Contract the muscles on the back of the shoulder to pull your arm or elbow further back and down for one to two seconds and then raise a straight or bent arm up to the vertical position. Lower under control until you once again feel a stretch. Contract your back muscles to pull the arm back and then raise it up to the vertical position. Repeat in a continuous manner. (See Fig. 5.10.)

11. Bent-Arm Elbow Raise. Assume a standing position with your arms alongside your body. When ready, bend one arm and raise the elbow as high as possible to the rear. Contract the shoulder muscles strongly to bring the elbow up as high as possible. Lower your arm or swing it forward. If you lower the arm, relax momentarily and then raise the elbow up

(a)

(b)

Figure 5.10   Arm flexion from a lying-back position

(a)

(b)

Figure 5.11   Bent-arm elbow raise

as high as possible in a continuous repetitive manner. If you swing the arm forward, then swing the bent arm back and hold the up position as you try to pull the elbow up as high as possible to the rear. Repeat in a continuous motion. Every time you raise the elbow try to go a little higher up to the rear. (See Fig. 5.11.)

Shoulder Elevation

Although shoulder elevation is not specific to improving running speed, it is important to prevent tightness in the upper back and neck area. This in turn allows for more natural and free

(a)

(b)

Figure 5.12 Shrug

running. The best exercise to improve this action is the shrug.

*12. **Shrug.*** To execute, assume a standing position with your shoulders relaxed and torso straight. When you are ready, raise your shoulders as high as possible while your arms are relaxed. If you have good flexibility, the shoulders will come up close to the level of your lower ears. After reaching the uppermost position, lower the shoulders completely and repeat in a rhythmical manner. (See Fig. 5.12.)

For immediate relaxation, raise your shoulders as high as possible, contract the muscles and feel them tighten for two to three seconds, and then quickly drop the shoulders to relax the muscles.

Jogging

Jogging is not a specific stretch but it is an excellent activity to warm up the muscles in preparation for your run. By jogging I mean starting the run very slowly and then gradually building up speed until you are ready to maintain your running tempo. Sprinters pick up their speed a little sooner. A short jog can precede the desired stretches, but jogging with a gradual buildup in speed should follow the stretches.

By doing these active stretches you activate the muscles much like the actions that occur in running. These stretches will help prevent injury, and most important, will greatly enhance your running.

6

Special Strength Exercises
for Running

Specialized exercises based on biomechanical and kinesiological analyses of effective running duplicate the exact movements, range of motion, and type of muscular contraction involved in running. In the initial stages of training, the exercises may not duplicate the *exact* muscular contraction because the body must first be prepared for some of these exercises. As a result, some of the exercises are done at different speeds or with slight modifications before duplicating the exact conditions seen in competitive running. By doing the exercises you will see immediate improvement in your running.

From a biomechanical analysis, it is possible to identify joint actions that are relatively weak, those that are executed effectively, and those needing modification. This information can help you select exercises that are most suitable to your abilities and can be instrumental in establishing your workout program. In essence, the analysis indicates the lagging aspects of your technique as well as the physical abilities that are lacking. Your training program should reflect these aspects so you can make the lagging areas commensurate with your strong points. You must also improve your strong points, especially if they are core movements. Thus the biomechani-

cal, and to a lesser extent the kinesiological, analysis is critical for you to become a better runner.

If you participate in a general conditioning program, you may see some progress when you get in better physical condition. But if the strength and other exercises do not duplicate what you do in running, or if the exercises do not enhance your strong or weak points, you will not see the improvement that is possible. The general physical preparation, however, serves as a strong base for doing the special exercises.

To strengthen the muscles as they are needed in running it is necessary to do a multitude of different exercises, especially when starting with general conditioning. You must involve all the major and minor muscles in many different exercises so the entire body is affected. Strengthening only the major muscles and ignoring some of the relatively minor muscles, especially of the foot, often leads to injury. Keep in mind that you are only as strong as your weakest link.

To greatly improve your running you must strengthen the muscles as they function in the key joint actions. Do at least one strength exercise for each major action involved. Also, use different speeds of execution to accustom your muscles to changes in running speed and to build greater overall strength.

Once your technique is determined you should do exercises to improve your technique as well as enhance your physical qualities. Since the key actions in running involve the agonist and the antagonist muscles you should do exercises for each set of muscles and for all the muscle-contraction regimes. Strengthening the muscles on both sides of the joint in all their actions to duplicate what occurs in the actual run prevents injury.

Following are some of the key strength exercises specific to running. Several variants of some exercises are presented to better fit the equipment available to you. Execution with rubber tubing is preferred if you work out at home or at the track. If you work out in a gym, execution on specialized equipment or free weights may be more appropriate.

Lower Body

1. Heel Raise. The purpose of this exercise is to strengthen the muscles that duplicate ankle-joint extension—the main action in the pushoff. The calves, which consist of the soleus and gastrocnemius muscles, are the major ones involved.

Execution with rubber tubing: On a stable board two to four inches high, stand on the balls of your feet so your heels are free to move. Using Active Cords with a belt attachment, secure the middle of the cord around and under the balls of your feet or under the platform or attachment board you are standing on. Then attach the ends of the tubing to the Active Cords belt fastened around your waist. Be sure there is adequate tension in the tubing. Keeping your legs straight, lower your heels until you feel a stretch in the Achilles tendon. Then rise up as high as possible and hold for one to two seconds. (See Fig. 6.1.) Lower your heels and repeat, going through a full range of motion on each repetition. If you have difficulty balancing yourself, hold on to a stationary object.

Execution in the gym: Place the balls of your feet on the raised platform and your shoulders under the resistance-lever pads of a calf-raise machine. Straighten your legs to assume a standing position. When you are ready, lower your heels until you feel a stretch of the Achilles tendon. Then rise up as high as possible and hold the up position for one to two seconds. (See Fig. 6.2.) Lower your heels and repeat. Inhale and hold your breath as you rise up, and exhale as you lower your body.

Change foot positions to develop some of the assisting muscles and to bring in other foot actions.

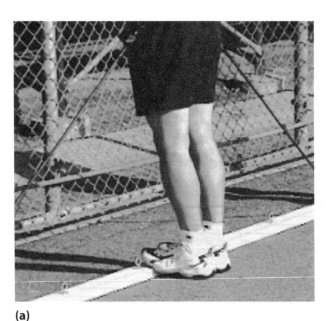
(a)

(b)

Figure 6.1   Heel raise using rubber tubing

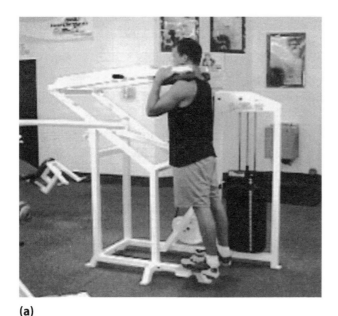 

(a) **(b)**

Figure 6.2 Heel raise using gym equipment

For example, point your toes inward for greater strengthening of the tibialis anterior. Position your toes outward to involve the three peroneal muscles and the extensor digitorum longus located on the lateral sides of the shins. Always keep your feet hip-width apart during execution.

To develop greater balance, do this exercise on a raised platform while holding dumbbells in your hands or a barbell across your shoulders. Execution is the same but, because of the balance factor, you may have to use less weight to maintain stability. If you need support, you can do the exercise on one leg in a stairway while you hold the handrail with one hand and a dumbbell in the other.

2. Toe Raise. This exercise contributes to raising the front part of the foot during the swing phase, helps prevent shin splints, and balances calf development. Note that the more you develop both the agonists and antagonists, the more development you can get out of either. Major muscles involved are the tibialis anterior, extensor digitorum longus, and peroneus tertius muscles, which are located on the front of the shin.

Execution with rubber tubing: Assume a seated position on the floor with the leg to be exercised extended and with one end of the Active Cord attached to the ball of the foot. The other end should

be secured at the same height, and there should be tension on the cord when you point the toes as far as possible away from yourself. When you are ready, pull the toe-ball area of the foot back toward the shin as far as possible. (See Fig. 6.3.) Hold for one or two seconds in the up position and then repeat.

Execution in the gym: The toe-raise exercise is done on a Tib Exerciser machine. Assume a seated position on an exercise bench and place your heels on the swivel heel plate of the machine. The toes should be placed under the resistance rollers with the foot angled downward as much as possible. When you are ready, raise your toes as high as possible. (See Fig. 6.4.) Hold for one to two seconds and then lower at a moderate rate of speed. Repeat after reaching the initial position. Note that you cannot raise the foot much above the horizontal position, so it is important that you go through the maximum range of motion from the extended ankle position. It is also more specific to running.

3. Seated Heel Raise (Seated Calf Raise). This exercise is designed to strengthen the soleus muscle, which is most important in endurance running but also plays an important role in sprinting, especially when trained explosively.

Execution with rubber tubing: Assume a seated position on the end of a bench so that the backs of

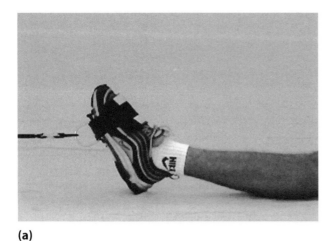
(a)

(b)

Figure 6.3   Toe raise using rubber tubing

(a)

(b)

Figure 6.4   Toe raise using gym equipment

your thighs are in full support. Your shins should hang straight down with the balls of the feet on a raised platform two to four inches high. Slip the two handles of the Active Cords on a pole placed across the tops of your thighs. The middle of the tubing should be wrapped around your feet under the balls. There should be tension on the cord in the starting position. When you are ready, raise your heel as high as possible against greater tension on the tubing. (See Fig. 6.5.) Hold for one to two seconds and then lower your heels so they are below the level of the balls of the feet. Then raise again and repeat in an alternating manner.

Execution in the gym: Assume a seated position on a seated calf machine and place the balls of your feet on the angled foot platform with your heels low and free to move. Pull the padded resistance bar over

your lower thighs and then release the weights so they are supported by your legs. Lower your heels to stretch the muscles and tendons and then raise them as high as possible. (See Fig. 6.6.) Hold the up position for one to two seconds and then relax slightly as you lower your heels under control to the original position below the level of the balls of the feet. Repeat when you are ready. For variety, change foot positions—point your toes inward or outward and then raise the heels.

4. Knee (Leg) Extension.   Knee extensions strengthen the quadriceps muscle group, with the primary goal of keeping the patella in its groove to prevent some of the more common knee injuries. (Full development of the quadriceps is best accomplished in the squat exercise.) The quadriceps also play the most

(a)

(b)

Figure 6.5 Seated heel raise using rubber tubing

(a)

(b)

Figure 6.6 Seated heel raise using gym equipment

important role in holding you upright and prevent you from "sitting" in the support phase.

Execution with rubber tubing: Assume a standing position facing away from the stationary attachment of the Active Cord. (Although leg extensions are typically done in a seated position, maintaining the thigh in a locked position creates great pressure on the knee joint during execution. Standing alleviates the stress and more closely duplicates the knee

extension as it occurs in the running stride.) With the other end of the rubber tubing attached to an ankle strap, raise your thigh to approximately a 45-degree angle. Hold the thigh in this position and then extend the leg against the resistance of the cord. Straighten the leg until it is completely extended and then relax, return to the original position, and repeat. You will notice that as you do this exercise there is slight movement of the thigh that acts as a

(a) **(b)**

Figure 6.7 Knee extension using rubber tubing

(a) **(b)**

Figure 6.8 Knee extension using gym equipment

safety valve for the knee joint and provides a more realistic action as occurs in sprinting. (See Fig. 6.7.)

Execution in the gym: Assume a seated position on a leg-extension machine so that your knees are at the end of the seat and your shins are against the inner-resistance arm rollers. Push against the rollers until your shins are at approximately a 90-degree angle to the thigh. This is the starting position. When you are ready, inhale slightly more than usual and hold your breath as you fully straighten your legs. (See Fig. 6.8.) Hold for one to two seconds and then relax and slowly return to the 90-degree angle position. For variety, do with toes in and toes out.

When doing knee extensions, it is important not to begin with the knee flexed less than 90 degrees (angle between back of thigh and shin). In this position the forces acting on the knee can be quite high

(a)

(b)

Figure 6.9 Knee extension using cable-pulley machine

and the exercise may be dangerous. When executed in the end range of motion, the exercise is effective in developing the two vasti muscles on the sides of the lower thigh that are most responsible for holding the patella in place.

Another variant of the knee extension can be executed in a gym using a cable machine such as the CMF. These units have a constant moving force (resistance) that can provide more effective development than a conventional cable machine. For more information, call 1-800-683-8360.

Execution is basically the same as with rubber tubing, however, using the CMF changes the point of resistance so you get more equal resistance distribution through the full range of motion. When using the CMF machine, be sure to hold your thigh at approximately a 45-degree angle as you swing out the shin until the knee is fully extended. Then hold your knee in place and bend your leg to return the shin to a position behind the thigh. (See Fig. 6.9.)

5. Knee (Leg) Curl.   Knee curls strengthen the hamstring muscles and the tendons that cross the knee joint, providing joint stability. The hamstring may be involved in raising the shin during the forward knee drive. Hamstring muscle development also is important in balancing the strength of the quadri-

ceps on the front of the thigh. The quadriceps should always be stronger, and although the exact ratio can vary, it appears to be close to three or four to one. Keep in mind that the stronger the hamstrings are, the more the quadriceps can be strengthened.

Execution with rubber tubing: Assume a standing position with the middle of the Active Cord looped around your foot or attached to the ankle strap on the leg to be exercised. The free end(s) of the cord should be secured under your other foot. When ready, hold your thigh vertical and bend the knee to bring the shin up to the level position. (See Fig. 6.10.) Return to the straight-leg position and repeat. Slight movement of the thigh is acceptable.

Execution in the gym: The knee-curl exercise can be done lying facedown or from a standing position. Most popular is the version in which you assume a facedown position so that your knees extend over the end of the angled bench and are free of support. The back of your lower legs (upper ankles) should rest against the underside of the resistance rollers. Hold the grips alongside the bench.

When you are ready, take a slightly greater than normal breath and hold your breath as you raise your feet by bending the knees. In the ending position your shins should be slightly past the vertical position. (See Fig. 6.11.) Exhale and relax the muscles

(a)

(b)

Figure 6.10   Knee curl using rubber tubing

(a)

(b)

Figure 6.11   Knee curl using gym equipment

slightly as you return to the original position under control, then repeat. Execute at a moderate rate of speed.

Another effective variant of the knee curl that can be executed in a gym is done on a cable-pulley machine such as the CMF unit. To execute, assume a standing position with your thigh horizontal and your knees slightly flexed. Place all your weight on one leg so that the leg to be exercised is free to move. Attach the ankle strap to the free end of the cable as you face the sliding resistance sleeve. When you are ready, bend your knee in a knee curling action until the shin is under the thigh and then return to the initial position; pause and then repeat. Execute at a moderate rate of speed. (See Fig. 6.12.) This variant can also be done with Active Cords.

6. Squat.   The purpose of the squat is to strengthen the anterior thigh muscles, which hold you upright during the support phase and prevent excessive sinking after touchdown. The squat is also one of the best exercises for preventing knee injuries.

(a)   **(b)**

Figure 6.12   Knee curl using cable-pulley machine

Major muscles involved are the quadriceps femoris muscle group.

Execution with rubber tubing: Place the middle of the Active Cord under both feet and hold the ends in your hands or attach to Active Cords belt. For greater resistance, hold the cord handles shoulder high in front of the body. When you are standing there should be strong tension on the cords. Stand with your feet approximately hip-width apart with your toes pointed straight ahead or turned out slightly. Inhale and hold your breath as you flex your knees and slowly lower your body into the squat position, keeping your heels in contact with the floor and the lower back in its normal curvature. Your knees should come forward slightly. Your buttocks should move slightly to the rear and then straight down, and your trunk should incline forward up to 45 degrees. Maintain a slight arch in the lower back at all times. After reaching the bottom position, reverse directions by forcefully extending the legs and rise up. (See Fig. 6.13.) When you pass the most difficult portion of the up phase, begin to

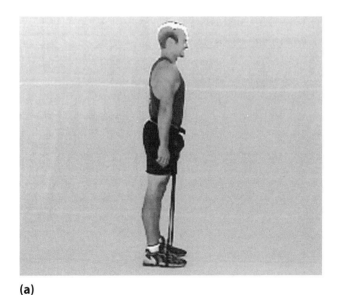

(a)   **(b)**

Figure 6.13   Squat using Active Cord

(a)

(b)

Figure 6.14 Squat using gym equipment

exhale, completing the exhalation when you are in a full standing position. Keep your eyes focused directly in front. The bottom position is determined by your ability to hold the arch in your lower back. If your spine begins to round in the down position, stop your descent immediately. The point at which back rounding occurs determines how far you lower your body.

Execution in the gym: Stand with your feet approximately shoulder-width apart and your toes pointed straight ahead or turned out slightly. Hold a barbell behind your neck across the shoulders, resting on the upper-trapezius muscle, or hold dumbbells in your hands. Execute the same as with rubber tubing. (See Fig. 6.14.) Repeat at a moderate rate of speed. For variety, lower the body at a moderate rate of speed, then rise up quickly.

7. Lunge. The goal of the lunge is to actively stretch the hip flexors for greater flexibility and stride length. Note that in the down position of the lunge you come close to duplicating the airborne position in sprinting.

Execution: Assume a well-balanced standing position with your feet hip-width apart. When you are ready, inhale and hold your breath as you step forward with a very long stride, keeping your trunk in a vertical position. Upon landing, hold the vertical trunk position and then slowly lower your upper body straight down. In the bottom position you should have approximately 90 degrees of flexion in your forward leg and most of your weight should be on it. Your rear leg should remain straight but relaxed. You should feel muscle tension in your front leg and lower back together with a strong stretch of the hip flexors of the rear leg. (See Fig. 6.15.)

After reaching the lowermost position, shift your weight backward and, as you do so, strongly extend your forward leg, then take several short steps to return to the original position. Exhale and repeat the exercise by stepping out with the other leg. Also effective is to rise up on the forward leg after each lunge (known as a walking lunge). This action strengthens the hip-extensor muscles.

When greater resistance is needed, hold your arms overhead, or hold a barbell across your chest or dumbbells in your hands. (See Fig. 6.16.) When you have developed sufficient hip-joint flexibility, the knee of your rear leg should almost touch the floor in the bottom position while the leg is kept straight.

8. Side Lunge. The side lunge stretches and strengthens the adductor muscles on the inner side of the thigh to prevent injury, stabilize the pelvis, and strengthen these muscles that contract in the initial movement of driving the thigh forward. This exercise is also important for athletes who must execute quick changes in direction (cutting) while running.

(a)

(b)

Figure 6.15 Lunge

Execution: Assume a comfortable standing position with your feet approximately hip-width apart. When you are ready, step out directly to the side and plant the foot at a 45-degree angle, keeping your trunk erect. Once the foot is firmly on the ground, lower your body directly downward until there is approximately a 90-degree angle in the lunging leg. The rear pushoff leg should remain straight and you should feel a strong stretch on the inner thigh. Hold for one to two seconds and then push off the forward foot to bring the weight backward. Rise up and repeat. (See Fig. 6.17.)

Figure 6.16 Variation on the lunge using dumbbells

When you have finished the desired number of repetitions with one leg, do the exercise with the other leg leading, or alternate legs. For greater resistance, hold dumbbells in your hands or a barbell across your shoulders. To increase difficulty and develop greater balance, hold your arms overhead with or without a barbell. (See Fig. 6.18.)

9. Forward Knee Drive (Hip-Joint Flexion).   This exercise duplicates the action of driving the thigh forward, which is important for increasing speed and stride length. Major muscles involved include the iliopsoas, pectineus, and the rectus femoris (when the knee is bent).

Execution with rubber tubing: Attach one end of the Active Cord to a stationary object about knee high and the other end behind your ankle. Stand far enough away so there is tension on the tubing when the leg is behind the body. Hold on to a partner or stationary object to stabilize your upper body. Your thigh should be free to move through a full range of motion. Your body should be erect and the leg to be exercised should be behind the body as far as possible to duplicate the thigh position immediately after pushoff. When you are ready, inhale slightly more than usual and hold your breath as you drive the thigh forward. Your knee should bend so that the shin remains basically parallel to the ground as the thigh is driven forward. Drive the thigh forward until it passes the vertical position. (See Fig. 6.19.)

(a)

Figure 6.17 Side lunge

(b)

Figure 6.18 Side lunge with arms raised

Do not drive the knee upward until the thigh is level to the parallel position. You want strength in the initial and following movement, which involves a powerful muscular contraction. After it passes the position slightly in front of the body, the thigh then moves on momentum to reach the uppermost thigh position. It is not important to develop strength through the full range of motion since that may teach you to drive the thigh upward rather than forward.

To duplicate more closely what occurs in running during the knee-drive phase, keep your trunk erect,

fully straighten the support leg, and rise up on the ball of your foot as you drive the knee forward. When you finish exercising with one leg, repeat with the opposite leg. Execute at a moderate rate of speed to develop greater strength. When your hip-flexor muscles become sufficiently strong, you can execute the exercise more forcefully, but again, only through a short range of motion. Begin the exercise with more tension on the tubing for more power. Add another cord for additional resistance rather than relying on greater stretch of the tubing.

Execution in the gym: This exercise can be executed on a CMF cable machine. Execution is the same as with rubber tubing, but be sure you have tension on the cable in the beginning position. (See Fig. 6.20.) This exercise can also be done on a multi-hip machine, but only if the axis of the machine lines up with the hip-joint axis. Also, the resistance pad should be close to the knee or the lower thigh when the leg is behind the body.

10. Pawback or Pullback (Hip-Joint Extension). This exercise duplicates the thigh pawback action—the down-and-back pulling action of the leg to make contact with the ground. This is a very important action for increasing stride length and running speed. Major muscles involved include the gluteus maximus and hamstring muscles and their ten-

(a)   **(b)**

Figure 6.19 Forward knee drive using rubber tubing

(a)   **(b)**

Figure 6.20 Forward knee drive using a cable-pulley machine

dons that cross the hip joints. Note that the upper-hamstring tendons are not worked when doing knee curls. Knee curls are essentially for knee stability while pawback is the key exercise that duplicates what occurs in the hip joint when running.

Execution with rubber tubing: Attach the Active Cord to a high stationary object. Attach the free end of the tubing to the front of the ankle of the leg to be exercised. Stand so that when the leg is raised, with the thigh slightly below parallel, the tubing is vertical. When you are ready, straighten the leg and pull down and back fairly vigorously. Initial ground contact

should be on the whole foot or the ball of the foot directly under the body. (See Fig. 6.21.)

Inhale and hold your breath as you pull down and back, and exhale and relax as you bring the leg back up in preparation for the next repetition. Balance your body in an erect stable position during execution. Initially you can hold on to something for greater stability, but as you become more confident, balance yourself as you execute the exercise.

Execution in the gym: Execution on a high-cable pulley is the same as with rubber tubing. However, care must be taken to accommodate movement

(a)

(b)

Figure 6.21 Pawback using rubber tubing

(a)

(b)

Figure 6.22 Pawback using a cable-pulley machine

of the weight stack, that is, you should stop after each repetition to allow the weights to return to position (except on the CMF unit, which has a stop). Be sure to maintain an erect trunk position and keep your leg straight as you pull down and back. (See Fig. 6.22.) This exercise can also be done on a multi-hip machine, but only if the axis of the machine lines up with the axis in the hip joint and you are able to straighten the leg during the pushing action. Begin with your thigh level, the knee bent slightly, and the trunk erect.

11. Hip-Joint Adduction.   This exercise strengthens the adductor muscles used in the initial part of the forward knee drive, improving your ability to make lateral movements and stabilize the pelvis. It also strengthens the medial collateral ligaments of the knee making it more stable.

Execution with rubber tubing: Stand with your feet apart, the inner leg to be exercised attached at the ankle to one end of the Active Cord. The other end should be attached to an immovable object close to the ground. When ready, shift your weight to the

(a)   **(b)**

Figure 6.23   Hip-joint adduction using rubber tubing

(a)   **(b)**

Figure 6.24   Hip-joint adduction using a cable-pulley machine

outside leg and then, keeping the leg to be exercised straight, pull the inside leg in to the other leg. (See Fig. 6.23.) Return to the initial position and repeat. Inhale and hold your breath as you pull the leg in, and exhale as you return to the initial position.

Execution in the gym: This exercise can also be effectively done on a low-cable pulley such as the CMF unit. Execution is the same as with rubber tubing. (See Fig. 6.24.) It is important that you have as straight a body as possible so that the muscular development is the same as occurs when the mus-

cles are used in running and for some athletes in cutting movements.

12. Hip-Joint Abduction. The abductor muscles hold level and stabilize the pelvis when running. This exercise may prevent certain knee problems by strengthening the lateral collateral ligament located on the outer sides of the knees.

Execution with rubber tubing: Attach the Active Cord to an ankle strap secured around the lower shin on the outside, with the other end

(a)　　　　　　　　　　　　　　　　**(b)**

Figure 6.25　Hip-joint abduction using rubber tubing

(a)　　　　　　　　　　　　　　　　**(b)**

Figure 6.26　Hip-joint abduction using a cable-pulley machine

secured to an immovable object close to the floor. Stand erect with your feet together and the leg to be exercised outermost. Hold something or someone about shoulder high to stabilize the upper body. When you are ready, straighten and hold the leg straight as you pull it out to the side as far as possible. Inhale and hold your breath to hold the upper body erect. Keep your toes pointed directly in front. (See Fig. 6.25.) After reaching the outermost position, exhale and return to the initial position under control. Pause momentarily and then repeat.

Execution in the gym: This exercise is executed the same as with rubber tubing on a low-cable pulley such as the CMF unit. (See Fig. 6.26.) The CMF unit provides more effective resistance through the full range of motion because of the moving resistance attachment.

13. The Good Morning.　The good morning increases stabilization strength of the lower back in its normal curvature, and stretches and strengthens the hamstring muscles and their upper tendons. Major

(a)

(b)

Figure 6.27 The good morning

muscles involved are the hamstrings, gluteus maximus, and lower-back muscles.

Execution: Stand erect with a barbell across your shoulders or dumbbells in your hands. Your feet should be approximately hip- to shoulder-width apart. Your legs should be straight or slightly bent and the lumbar spine should be in its normal alignment, i.e., with a slight arch at all times. When you are ready, inhale slightly more than usual and hold your breath as you bend forward from the hip joints. Push your hips backward as your trunk inclines forward and down to the horizontal position (or as far as your flexibility will allow). Do not round the back! After reaching the lowermost position (when you feel a tightness in the hamstrings), reverse directions and rise up to the starting position. Exhale as you approach the upright position. (See Fig. 6.27.) Relax momentarily and then repeat.

14. Glute-Ham-Gastroc Raise. The purpose of this exercise is to provide maximum strengthening of the hamstring muscles and their tendons at the hip joint as well as the knee joint. This exercise has proved to be exceptionally valuable for runners in preventing and rehabilitating hamstring injuries. In my experience, no athlete or sprinter has had a hamstring injury when this exercise has been executed on a regular basis. In addition, the hamstring

muscles are developed through the same range of motion and action used in running.

Execution: I introduced this exercise to the running world. It is executed on the Yessis Back Machine, also known as the glute-ham machine, which I created for this exercise. Assume a facedown position so support is on the upper thighs when your feet are placed between the rear rollers. When your legs are in place, lower your trunk over and down the front side of the seat and hold the back in its normal curvature. Your upper body and pelvic girdle should form a straight line from the hip joint to the head. Inhale slightly more than usual and hold your breath as you raise your trunk with the axis in the hips. Your back should remain rigid in its slightly arched position. Raise your trunk until the body forms a straight line from your head to your feet. Then keep the hip-joint extensor muscles under contraction and bend your knees. Keep raising your straight body (from your knees to your head) to approximately a 30-degree angle above the horizontal. (See Fig. 6.28.)

After reaching the top position, exhale and relax slightly but keep the lower back in its slightly arched position. Lower your body by straightening your legs and then flexing at the hips to return to the original position. Execute the exercise at a moderate rate of speed.

(a)   **(b)**

(c)

Figure 6.28   The glute-ham-gastroc raise using the Yessis Back Machine

The Midsection

The midsection includes the abdominal and lower-back muscles. The lower-back muscles are responsible for maintaining the erect running posture, and the abdominals (mainly the internal and external obliques) play an important role in preventing excess hip and shoulder rotation. The lower-abdominal muscles (mainly the lower portion of the rectus abdominis) play a very important role in rotating the pelvis backward to enhance the knee drive and to create a longer stride length, which is especially important in sprinting.

Abdominal Exercises

In running, the internal and external obliques are used to prevent shoulder and hip rotation, but they also play a very important role in forced exhalation.

This is especially important for sprinters. The most powerful muscle in forced expiration, however, is the transverse abdominis. This is the deepest abdominal muscle and is not involved in trunk movement. Its main function is forced expiration and, since it is the deepest layer of abdominal muscle, it holds in the abdominal viscera. The lower portion of the rectus abdominis is important in sprinting as it rotates the pelvis to allow for a full and powerful knee drive.

15. Reverse Sit-Up. This exercise strengthens mainly the lower portion of the rectus abdominis, which is involved in posterior pelvic-girdle rotation. This action is needed in the forward knee drive. The external and internal obliques are also involved.

Execution: Lie on your back with your arms alongside your body and your feet off the floor, knees bent and thighs vertical. This is the starting position. When you are ready, inhale slightly more

(a)

(b)

Figure 6.29 Reverse sit-up

Figure 6.30 Reverse sit-up with arms raised overhead

than usual and then hold your breath as you rotate the pelvis up and toward the shoulders until your hips are off the ground. Keep your knees bent tightly as you do this so the action is isolated to the lower abdominals. (See Fig. 6.29.) Push down with your hands to raise your hips (and legs), and to ensure adequate rotation of the pelvic girdle. In the ending position your knees should be chest high. Keep your head and shoulders relaxed throughout the upward movement. Exhale as you return to the initial position, pause, and then repeat.

When doing the exercise in this manner becomes easy, place your arms over your head so they cannot assist in execution. Then do the exercise concentrating on only the lower abdominals to rotate the

hips upward. To involve more of the upper portion of the abdominal muscles, continue rotating your pelvis and legs up and over until your knees are close to your head. This is a more advanced movement and one in which you get more dynamic stretching of the lower back. (See Fig. 6.30.)

16. Reverse Trunk Twist. The reverse trunk twist improves midsection flexibility and strengthens the internal and external obliques in a rotary action to prevent rotation while running. This exercise is especially important for open-field runners who must execute quick changes in direction to elude their opponents. It is also a great back stretch.

Execution: Lie faceup on the floor with your arms out to the sides and palms down. Your arms should be perpendicular to your trunk so your body forms a letter T. Raise your legs (thighs) to a 90-degree angle from the floor. Then lower your legs to one side while continuing to hold the 90-degree angle in the hip joints. Touch the floor with the outside of your lower foot if you keep your legs relatively straight (more difficult), or with the outer knee if you keep your legs bent. Keep your shoulders and arms in full contact with the floor. Inhale and hold your breath as you raise your legs back up to the initial position and, without stopping, over to the opposite side until you touch the floor once again. (See Fig. 6.31.) Exhale as you lower your legs and then inhale and hold as you raise them. Execute alternating sides on each repetition.

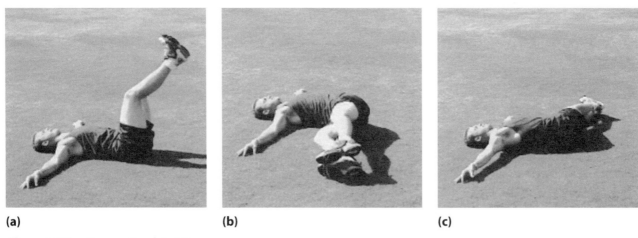

(a)   **(b)**   **(c)**

Figure 6.31   Reverse trunk twist

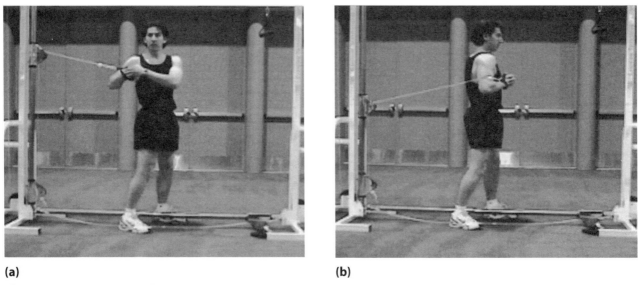

(a)   **(b)**

Figure 6.32   Reverse trunk twist using a cable-pulley machine

A variant of the reverse trunk twist can also be done in the gym by doing shoulder rotations on a cable machine such as the CMF unit. Face away from the moving resistance attachment and hold the cable handle in both hands at one shoulder. Begin with your shoulders rotated to the rear approximately 90 degrees. When you are ready, inhale and hold your breath as you rotate the shoulders forward or slightly beyond the front-facing position. Exhale and return to the initial position. Repeat at a moderate rate of speed. (See Fig. 6.32.) This exercise can also be done with rubber tubing.

17. Yessis Back Machine Sit-Up.   This exercise strengthens the hip flexors and abdominals, especially the lower abdominals, as they are used in running. This exercise is especially important for sprinters.

Execution Variant 1: Adjust the Yessis Back Machine so that, when you are seated on the rounded pad, support will be on the buttocks. Your feet should be between the back rollers and your legs fully extended. Inhale slightly more than usual and hold your breath as you lower your trunk back and down until it is slightly below the level of your thighs. Your legs should remain straight at all times. When you are in the correct position, you will feel

(a)

(b)

Figure 6.33 Yessis Back Machine sit-up, variant 1

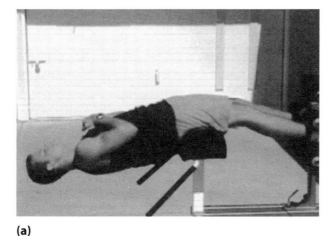

(a)

(b)

Figure 6.34 Yessis Back Machine sit-up, variant 2

tension mainly in the abdominal muscles and some tension in the hip and thigh muscles.

After reaching the down position, keep holding your breath and curl your trunk up to about 45 degrees above level or to the full upright seated position. (See Fig. 6.33.) Use mainly the abdominals to return to the upright position at which time you should exhale quickly. When you are ready to repeat, inhale and return back down. Be sure to keep your legs straight as you execute this exercise. This will prevent you from going too low or excessively hyperextending the spine.

Execution Variant 2: Adjust the Yessis Back Machine so that when you are seated on the rounded pad, support will be on the back of your upper thighs and buttocks. Your feet should be between the rollers and your legs fully extended. Inhale slightly more than usual and hold your breath as you lower your trunk back and down until it is slightly below the level of your thighs. Your legs should remain straight at all times. When you are in the correct position, you will feel tension in the abdominal, hip, and thigh muscles. After reaching the down position, keep holding your breath and

(a)

(b)

Figure 6.35   Resistive breathing

curl your trunk up to about 30 degrees. Use your hip flexors and lower abdominals to return to the upright position and then exhale. (See Fig. 6.34.) Be sure to keep your legs straight as you execute this exercise so you do not lower your body down too far or excessively hyperextend the spine.

18. Resistive Breathing.   Resistive breathing strengthens the inspiratory and expiratory muscles to delay the onset of fatigue, improve cardiovascular endurance, and increase VO_2 max. Major muscles involved in inspiration are the diaphragm and intercostals. Those involved in expiration are the internal and external obliques and the transverse abdominis.

Execution: To most effectively strengthen the respiratory muscles you must use a resistive device such as the Breather. With this device you can adjust the resistance for inhalation and exhalation to better match your capabilities. To exercise the muscles, forcefully inhale against the resistance and then exhale against resistance at a steady rhythm for up to one minute. Then relax for a minute and repeat. (See Fig. 6.35.)

Breathing can be modified to match different conditions. For example, in sprinting where there is some breath-holding, you can forcefully inhale, hold the breath, forcefully exhale, and so on. Since one of the key actions in breathing is forceful exhalation you should concentrate on greater development of this ability. The faster and more forcefully you can get air out, the quicker you can take air in for a more effective exchange of gases in the lungs.

Strengthening the respiratory muscles is also very beneficial to runners and athletes who have asthma.

Lower-Back Exercises

The most important muscles of the lower back are the erector spinae and the quadratus lumborum, a deep muscle located on the sides of the lumbar spine. The erector spinae runs the length of your spine from the pelvis to your head. Its main function is to raise the trunk and keep you in the vertical position while you are running. The quadratus lumborum is most important for lateral stability of the spine. The following exercises develop these muscles for prevention and rehabilitation of many back problems.

19. Back Raise.   The back raise strengthens the lower-back muscles through the full range of motion. For runners it is very important to have strong lower-back muscles to maintain an erect trunk position while running. The back raise is also the best exercise to prevent back injury by strengthening the erector spinae and the small deep-back muscles involved in extension and hyperextension.

Execution: Back raises are most conveniently and safely done on the Yessis Back Machine. (If this machine is not available, you can use a high sturdy table and an assistant to hold down your legs.) Position yourself facedown over the curved seat of the Yessis Back Machine so that when your feet are

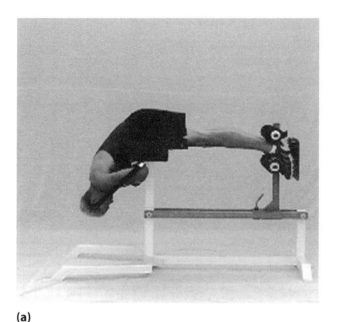

(a)

(b)

Figure 6.36 Back raise

placed between the rear pads your entire pelvic girdle rests on the seat. Lower your upper trunk over the seat and relax the spinal muscles. In this position your spine will naturally assume a rounded position and will be at approximately a 60-degree angle below the horizontal. Your legs should be fully extended and kept straight at all times. From the down position, inhale slightly more than usual and hold your breath as you extend (straighten) your spine to raise the upper body until it is slightly higher than your legs, i.e., so that there is a slight arch in the lower back. (See Fig. 6.36.) After reaching the uppermost position hold for one to two seconds and then exhale and return to the original position under control. When you reach the lowermost position, relax your muscles and then repeat.

20. Reverse Back Raise. If you are uncomfortable with your trunk in an upside-down position, do the reverse back raise. In this exercise you position yourself in the opposite manner on the Yessis Back Machine. The abdomen should be directly on top of the rounded seat and your legs should hang down at approximately a 60-degree angle. Your hands should hold the back plate or rollers to stabilize the upper body. When you are ready, inhale and raise your legs until they are above the level of the trunk, then exhale as you lower your legs, and repeat. (See Fig. 6.37.)

For greater resistance use the Active Cord. Place the attachment board under the front supports of the machine to secure it and attach both ends of the rubber tubing to the hook directly under the legs. Wrap the middle of the cord around one or both legs. There should be slight tension on the tubing when you are in the down position. When you are ready, inhale and hold your breath as you raise your leg(s) until it is in line with or slightly higher than the level of your back. Then exhale and return to the initial position. Relax for a moment and then repeat. Be sure to keep your legs straight during execution. (See Fig. 6.38.)

21. Side Bend. Side bends help hold the body erect in the lateral plane and avoid excessive bending to one side or the other. This is the main exercise that strengthens the quadratus lumborum, a key muscle in the lower back. Other muscles involved are the internal and external obliques, and the erector spinae and rectus abdominis on the side being exercised.

Execution with rubber tubing: Assume a standing position with feet shoulder-width apart. Hold one end of the Active Cord in one hand with the other hand alongside your body or behind your head. The other end of the cord should be under your feet, and there should be tension on the tubing

(a)

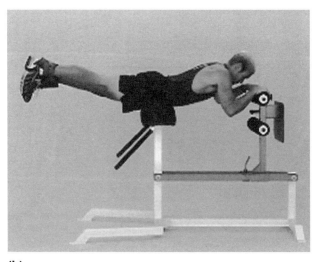

(b)

Figure 6.37 Reverse back raise

in the starting position. Keep your weight equally balanced on both feet and your pelvic girdle firmly in place. When you are ready, lower your shoulders and upper trunk to the same side as the tubing as far as possible without shifting your pelvis to the other side. Upon reaching the bottom position, inhale and hold your breath as you raise your trunk sideways back to the erect standing position and over to the other side as far as possible. (See Fig. 6.39.) Exhale as you return to the starting position and then repeat.

Execution in the gym: Hold a dumbbell in one hand and execute in the same manner as with rubber tubing. Use a moderately heavy weight for suffi-

Figure 6.38 Reverse back raise with aid of rubber tubing

cient resistance. (See Fig. 6.40.) Side bends can also be done using a low-pulley cable such as the CMF unit. Execution is the same as with rubber tubing or a dumbbell. (See Fig. 6.41.)

The Upper Body

In the upper body it is most important to strengthen the muscles involved in driving the arms forward in synchronization with the thighs. Long-distance runners should develop more muscular endurance of the arm and shoulder muscles to hold the bent-elbow position and to move the arm forward and backward throughout the run. For sprinters it is important to strengthen the arm and shoulder muscles to drive the arms forward and downward for greater loading of the leg muscles on contact with the ground.

Strengthening exercises are also needed to maintain the shoulders in position to prevent crossing the arms and to keep the chest cage elevated and expanded to allow for better breathing. In addition, strengthening the respiratory muscles is very important. (See Exercise 18.)

22. Bent-Arm Forward Raise. The purpose of this exercise is to strengthen the muscles involved in driving the arms forward during the pushoff phase and to increase shoulder flexibility. Major muscles

(a)

(b)

(c)

Figure 6.39 Side bend using rubber tubing

(a)

(b)

Figure 6.40 Side bend using gym equipment

(a)

(b)

Figure 6.41 Side bend using a cable-pulley machine

involved are the anterior deltoid, the upper portion of the pectoralis major muscle of the chest, and the biceps brachii of the upper arm.

Execution with rubber tubing: Hold the handle of the Active Cord and face away from the stationary attachment behind the body. Straighten your arm while still maintaining a slight bend in the elbow joint and with the arm slightly behind the body. When you are ready, begin pulling the arm forward and, as you do so, begin bending the elbow. Maintain the forward arm drive and continue bending your arm until the elbow is alongside or slightly in front of your body and your hand is approximately shoulder high. (See Fig. 6.42.) Have the other arm

work in synchronization with the arm being worked. Do only one arm at a time. When you finish the repetitions with one arm, execute with the opposite arm.

Execution in the gym: Use a cable apparatus such as the CMF machine that allows the point of resistance to move the arm as it comes forward. To execute, assume an upright position with the arm behind the body, as with the rubber tubing, and pull the arm through in a similar manner. Stop when the elbow is alongside or slightly in front of your body and your hand is approximately shoulder high. Straighten your arm as you return to the initial position, and repeat. (See Fig. 6.43.)

(a)

(b)

Figure 6.42 Bent-arm forward raise using rubber tubing

(a)

(b)

Figure 6.43 Bent-arm forward raise using gym equipment

23. Rear Elbow Raise (Shoulder-Joint Extension). This exercise strengthens the muscles involved in raising the elbow up in the rear, including the posterior deltoid and the long head of the triceps brachii.

Execution with rubber tubing: Assume a standing positioin holding the Active Cord handle at one end of the rubber tubing, with the other end secured under your feet. When you are ready, inhale and hold your breath as you raise your elbow as high as possible to the rear. Do not use too much resistance as it may limit your range of motion. The elbow should come up to approximately shoulder level.

(See Fig. 6.44.) After reaching the uppermost position, exhale and return to the initial position, pause momentarily and then repeat. Be sure to do this exercise with both arms.

Execution with gym equipment: This exercise can also be done in the gym using a low-cable pulley such as the CMF unit. Execute the same as with rubber tubing. Be sure you are capable of raising your elbow all the way up so that it is fairly close to level while you maintain the erect trunk position. Pause momentarily in the bottom position with a straight arm before repeating. (See Fig. 6.45.)

(a)

(b)

Figure 6.44 Rear elbow raise using rubber tubing

(a)

(b)

Figure 6.45 Rear elbow raise using gym equipment

24. *Standing Horizontal Pull.* The purpose of this exercise is to strengthen the muscles on the back of the shoulder and the middle of the back in order to keep the scapula (shoulder blades) in close to the spine. This in turn keeps the shoulders back in good posture and allows the arms to move directly forward and back. Note that if the shoulders are slightly forward (rounded), the arms will have a tendency to cross in front of the body. This exercise strengthens the rhomboid and the middle portion of the trapezius in the mid-back as well as the muscles of the shoulder, which keep the shoulders and arms in proper position.

Execution with rubber tubing: Attach one end of the Active Cord to a post approximately shoulder high or somewhat above. Hold the handle at the other end of the tubing in your hand and stand facing the attachment at an angle to the side. The arm holding the handle of the rubber tubing should cross the front of the body slightly. When you are ready, inhale and hold your breath as you bend your arm and pull the elbow back and to the rear as far as possible. (See Fig. 6.46.) You will notice that the shoulder also retracts to the rear as the elbow goes back. After reaching the back position, return to the initial position and relax for a moment and then repeat. Go through a full range of motion, allowing the shoulder to become rounded in the forward move-

ment and then be pulled all the way back as you pull the rubber tubing to the rear. The key is to pull with the muscles in the middle of the back and behind the shoulder. Repeat in an alternating manner.

Execution in the gym: The standing horizontal pull can also be duplicated on a high-pulley cable machine such as the CMF unit. Execution is exactly the same as with rubber tubing. (See Fig. 6.47.)

25. *Narrow-Grip Lat Pulldown.* This exercise is especially important for sprinters. It is used to develop the muscles involved in pulling the arm down (along with elbow extension) to create greater loading of the leg muscles as the foot makes contact with the ground. For long-distance runners (and sprinters) this exercise is needed to strengthen the muscles involved in pulling the arm to the rear in the initial movement. Major muscles involved include the latissimus dorsi, lower pectoralis major, and teres major.

Execution with rubber tubing: Attach one end of the Active Cord to a high post so that when you hold the other end in your hand your arm will be fully extended when you feel some tension on the tubing. If you cannot get the attachment very high, assume a kneeling position to get ample stretch of the tubing. When you are ready, hold your arm straight and pull straight down until your hand is

(a)   **(b)**

Figure 6.46 Standing horizontal pull using rubber tubing

(a)

(b)

Figure 6.47 Standing horizontal pull using a cable-pulley machine

alongside your body. (See Fig. 6.48.) Return to the initial position and repeat. Inhale and hold your breath as you pull your arm down, and exhale and relax (while still controlling the movement) as your arm returns to the up position. Do each repetition as a single movement, concentrating on pulling the arm down as occurs in running. Do the exercise with both arms.

Execution in the gym: Grasp a lat pulldown machine or high-pulley cable bar with a pronated grip, your elbows bent 90 degrees and pointed forward. Your hands should be approximately shoul-

der-width apart. Inhale and hold your breath as you pull the bar down at a moderate rate of speed. Concentrate on keeping your elbows in position and your trunk erect. Keep pulling down until the bar is chest high and your elbows are alongside your chest. (See Figs. 6.49 and 6.50.) Exhale as you return to the initial position. For increased difficulty, do the exercise with straight arms.

26. The Pullover. The pullover expands the chest to allow for fuller lung action. This improves your breathing capabilities. Major muscles involved

(a)

(b)

Figure 6.48 Narrow-grip lat pulldown using rubber tubing

(a)   **(b)**

Figure 6.49   Narrow-grip lat pulldown using gym equipment

(a)   **(b)**

Figure 6.50   Narrow-grip lat pulldown using a cable-pulley machine

include the lower portion of the pectoralis major, the latissimus dorsi, and the teres major.

Execution with rubber tubing: Assume a faceup position on the ground, holding one end of the Active Cord in both hands. Arms should be fully extended above your head and resting on the ground. The other end of the tubing should be attached to a low stationary object close to the ground. When you are ready, inhale deeply, hold your breath, and pull your straight arms up until they are above your chest. Exhale and then, when

ready to repeat, inhale deeply and hold your breath as you lower your arms back down to the ground. (See Figure 6.51.) Be sure to take as deep a breath as possible as you lower your arms. When your arms reach ground level, continue to hold your breath and pull your arms up until they are again above your chest. Repeat at a moderate rate of speed.

Execution in the gym: Lie faceup on an exercise bench so that you are well balanced with your trunk and pelvic girdle on the bench and your feet flat on the floor. Your body should be positioned so that your

(a)

(b)

Figure 6.51 The pullover using rubber tubing

(a)

(b)

Figure 6.52 The pullover using gym equipment

elbows clear the end of the bench when your upper arms are directly overhead (back). With your arms straight, hold a dumbbell above your chest. Hold the inner plate of the dumbbell so that the shaft remains vertical throughout the movement. Lower the dumbbell over your head and down until your upper arms are in line with your trunk. (See Fig. 6.52.)

A slightly lower position can be attained if you have the needed shoulder-joint flexibility. As you lower the weight, take a deep breath to greatly expand the rib cage. When you reach the lowermost position, keep holding your breath and then raise the dumbbell until it is above your chest. Exhale as you approach the vertical position. Pause momentarily and then repeat. To get maximum benefit from this exercise, use abdominal breathing so there is greater expansion of the lower rib cage.

27. Biceps Curl. The goal of the biceps curl is to hold the elbow at approximately a 90-degree angle during long-distance running for greater economy. In sprinting this exercise is needed to attain the 90-degree angle in the elbow joint as the arm is driven forward.

Execution with rubber tubing: Assume a well-balanced standing position with your feet approximately shoulder-width apart. Hold the Active Cord handle with a neutral (palm facing inward with the thumb uppermost) grip and with your hand in line with your shoulder. Extend your arm fully with your elbows free or lightly touching the sides of your body. Keep your chest high and your shoulders back. Inhale slightly more than usual and hold your breath as you execute the curling action. Keep your shoulder and elbow in position at all times as you raise your hand to shoulder level. (See Fig. 6.53.) After reaching the uppermost position, hold for one to two seconds and then exhale and return under control to the starting position. Relax for a moment and then repeat.

Execution in the gym: There are many variants of the biceps curl that can be done in the gym. The simplest is to use dumbbells and execute the same as with rubber tubing, keeping the neutral grip throughout execution. Flex the elbow until you have 90 degrees or slightly less of flexion in the elbow joint. (See Fig. 6.54.)

The biceps curl can also be done on a low-pulley cable apparatus. It is executed in basically the same manner as with the rubber tubing. When using a CMF unit, you get movement of the resistance attachment to keep the resistance strong throughout the entire range. Be sure to maintain an erect body position as you execute these variants. (See Fig. 6.55.)

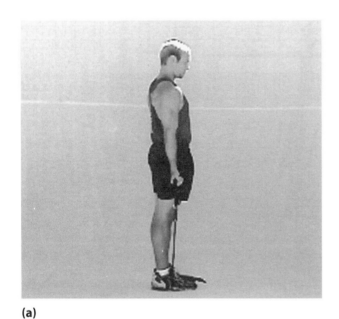
(a)

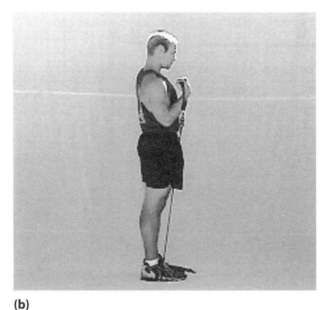
(b)

Figure 6.53   Biceps curl using rubber tubing

(a)

(b)

Figure 6.54   Biceps curl using gym equipment

28. Triceps Extension (Triceps Pushdown). This exercise is used to create more force for the arm-straightening action (throwing the hand toward the ground at touchdown) by sprinters.

Execution with rubber tubing: Stand in a well-balanced position with your feet approximately shoulder-width apart. Position yourself in front of the Active Cord, which is attached to a high beam or post. Assume a neutral grip (palm facing inward and with your elbow alongside your body). Begin the exercise with your hand slightly above elbow level so there is less than 90 degrees of flexion in the elbow joint. Inhale and hold your breath as you push down with your hand to extend your arm. Hold your elbow in place, keeping your grip firm and your hand and forearm in a straight line as you pull down. Continue extending the elbow until your arm is straight. (See Fig. 6.56.) After reaching this position, relax the muscles somewhat and then return to the original position and repeat.

Execution in the gym: The triceps extension is executed in a gym on a high-pulley cable such as on the CMF unit, or a lat pulldown machine (using both arms). Execute in exactly the same manner as with rubber tubing. Be sure to maintain a straight body

(a)

(b)

Figure 6.55 Biceps curl using a cable-pulley machine

(a)

(b)

Figure 6.56 Triceps extension using rubber tubing

(a)

(b)

Figure 6.57 Triceps extension using gym equipment

position as you execute and fully control the movement on the return. (See Fig. 6.57.)

29. Triceps Kickback. This is an alternate for the triceps pushdown and arm-pull exercises. Its purpose is to duplicate the arm-straightening action, especially raising the elbow behind the body, during recovery phase. It also involves the posterior deltoid.

Execution: Bend over from the hips so that your trunk is basically horizontal (almost parallel to the ground). Your feet should be flat on the ground in a stride stance and your knees should be bent with the trunk supported by the nonexercising arm. Hold a dumbbell with a neutral grip and bend your arm so your upper arm is alongside your body and your

forearm hangs down or is slightly under your arm. In the gym you can support your upper body with your free arm placed on the bench. When you are ready, inhale slightly more than usual and hold your breath as you extend your arm until it is straight. Keep your elbow in place as you move your hand with the weight backward and upward in an arc of a circle. After your arm is fully extended, pause momentarily, then raise the arm upward as far as possible so that in the final position the dumbbell is above the level of your back, which should remain in position. (See Fig. 6.58.) Exhale and return to the initial position under control, and repeat. Execute this exercise in two actions: straighten the arm and then raise it as high as possible.

(a)

(b)

(c)

Figure 6.58 Triceps kickback

30. Shrug. Shrugs strengthen the muscles involved in holding the shoulders up and prevent excessive tightness of the upper trapezius while running.

Execution with rubber tubing: Hold the handles attached to the Active Cords alongside your body with the middle of the tubing under or wrapped around your feet to create sufficient tension. When you are ready, keep your arms relaxed, then inhale slightly more than usual and hold your breath as you raise your shoulders as high as possible. Your shoulders should come close to the bottoms of your ears. (See Fig. 6.59.) Note that the exact height depends on your neck length. Pause momen-

tarily and then lower your shoulders under control to the initial position. Tense the muscles in the up phase and exhale and relax the muscles in the down phase.

Execution in the gym: The shrug is most effectively done with dumbells in the gym. To execute, assume a standing position holding a dumbell in each hand. When ready, relax the shoulders so they reach their lowermost position, then inhale and hold your breath as you raise your shoulders as high as possible. (See Fig. 6.60.) Pause momentarily and then lower your shoulders under control to the initial position. Repeat when ready.

(a)

(b)

Figure 6.59 Shrug using rubber tubing

(a)

(b)

Figure 6.60 Shrug using gym equipment

7

Explosive Exercises for Running

The explosive power seen in sprinting comes mainly from the leg actions. To increase the ability of the leg muscles to contract explosively, it is necessary to do strength exercises in combination with speed and quickness exercises (speed-strength exercises). This is the key to increasing explosive power and running speed.

Before undertaking speed and explosive training (sometimes called plyometric training) to increase running speed, you must have an adequate warm-up. One of the best ways is to do some jogging, active stretches (described in Chapter 5), and various kinds of easy jumps. After jogging and active stretching, start off with easy low-height jumps and gradually build up height and intensity until you are ready for all-out explosive jumps.

Speed-strength or explosive training most often entails some form of jumping, and how you jump is critical to your development. When you do easy jump activities, such as simple hopping and skipping, technique is not critical. But as the jumps become more powerful, higher, and longer, then how you take off and land becomes extremely important to your development and for injury prevention. Fig. 7.1 shows a landing, takeoff, and another landing.

General Characteristics of Jumping

The Takeoff

Jumping requires the coordinated action of the legs, trunk, and arms. Before jumping upward, you must first go into a partial squat by flexing at the ankle, knee, and hip joints. (See Fig. 7.1 frames d, e.) In this slight crouch, you place the extensor muscles that are used in the upward jump on eccentric stretch. The eccentric contraction switches to an isometric contraction when the downward movement is stopped in preparation for the upward (takeoff) movement, at which time the muscular contraction switches to concentric. The faster the changes in these muscular contractions take place, the higher you will jump and the more forceful and explosive will be the muscular contraction.

As you approach the bottom position, you whip your arms down and then up. (See Fig. 7.1 frames e–g.) The bottom arc of this arm movement places a greater load on your leg muscles so they contract with even more force in the takeoff. When you then raise your arms and trunk, you raise the body's center of gravity and your body becomes momentarily

107

(a)

(b)

(c)

(d)

(e)

(f)

(g)

(h)

(i)

(j)

(k)

(l)

(m)

(n)

(o)

Figure 7.1 Form for jumping and landing

lighter. The muscles now contract with greater force and propel you higher because you are lighter.

As you straighten your legs in the jump, the leg actions overlap one another to some extent. The first action to take place should be hip extension, followed by knee extension, and then ankle extension. The ankle-joint extension should be last because it contributes substantial force to the jump after the body is completely extended. As you leave the ground, your legs should be fully straightened, the trunk should be straight in line with the legs, and the arms can either be overhead or shoulder level. (See Fig. 7.1 frames f–k.)

In the initial stance, your feet should be placed directly under your hips so that when you straighten your legs they push the hips and upper body straight upward. If you place your feet wider than hip-width apart, when your legs extend the forces created will cross your body. As a result, only a portion of the forces generated will be used to raise your body. The remaining force will be wasted since it goes sideways.

The Landing

When preparing for touchdown, your feet should be directly under your hips so that the landing forces can be handled efficiently by the leg muscles. Landing should take place on the ball of the foot, followed immediately by the heel (unless you have exceptional calf strength). This is followed in turn by ankle-, knee-, and hip-joint flexion. Do not land with your toes pointed so that you land on the toes. This position can cause excessive jamming of the foot bones that can create various foot problems. The key to a safe and effective touchdown is to land with the underside of the foot approximately 45 degrees to the horizontal so that the ball-heel contact occurs very quickly. This allows for the arch of the foot to absorb the initial shock and, more important, to withstand most of the landing forces. This is not only the most effective form of landing, but one that will prevent injury. (See Fig. 7.1 frames a–d.)

To ensure an effective and safe landing, you should tense your foot and leg muscles slightly while you are still in the air. In other words, men-tally and physically prepare for touchdown before actually making contact. (See Fig. 7.1 frames n, o.) When you do this, as soon as you make initial contact, the muscles and tendons will be engaged immediately and will keep you from going too low and dissipating the forces generated. In fact, the less you go down and the faster you leave the ground, the higher you jump. This is due to energy accumulated from the forces withstood for giveback in the takeoff. This ability to accumulate energy and to quickly give it back is the key to increased running speed and being able to leap very quickly.

Explosive Strength Exercises

1. Explosive Heel Raise. This exercise develops an explosive muscle contraction as used in the pushoff. It involves the calf muscles.

Execution: Execution is basically the same as in the heel-raise strength exercise, except for the speed of execution. When positioned with the balls of your feet on the foot platform, inhale slightly more than usual and hold your breath as you lower your heels at a moderate rate of speed. As soon as you feel a strong stretch on the Achilles tendon, quickly reverse directions and rise up as high as possible. (See Fig. 7.2.) Hold the up position for one to two seconds, and then exhale and repeat. Be sure to make the transition from the down movement to the up movement as fast as possible. The range of movement is slightly less than when doing the exercise slowly.

2. Explosive Seated Calf Raise. This exercise trains the soleus muscle to contract in a more explosive manner.

Execution: Execution is basically the same as in the seated calf-raise strength exercise, except for speed of execution. Lower your heels at a moderate rate of speed, and as soon as you feel a strong stretch on the Achilles tendon, quickly reverse directions. Fully extend your ankle and hold the up position for one to two seconds. (See Fig. 7.3.) Pause between repetitions, and concentrate on a quick change in direction.

(a)

(b)

Figure 7.2   Explosive heel raise

(a)

(b)

Figure 7.3   Explosive seated calf raise

3. Squat Jump. Squat jumps develop greater eccentric strength to stop the down action of the body upon landing and develop a more powerful takeoff. Major muscles involved are the same as in the squat and heel raise.

Execution: Assume a standing position with your feet directly under your hips and hold a dumbbell in each hand, with arms extended. When you are ready, bend your knees and go into a slight crouch and then explode upward as high as possible. Be sure your ankles are fully extended and your legs are straight on takeoff. Prepare for landing as you are coming down and then, immediately after touchdown, absorb some of the shock but withstand the landing forces in a minimal crouch. (See Fig. 7.4.) Immediately jump up again as high as possible. Be sure you inhale and hold your breath during landing and takeoff, and exhale quickly when

(a)   **(b)**   **(c)**

Figure 7.4   Squat jump

you are airborne. Quickly inhale as you prepare to land and repeat this breathing pattern in synchronization with the jumping.

4. Split Squat Jump. This exercise develops a quicker and more forceful takeoff. It is very important for open-field runners who must make quick changes in direction, especially in forward and backward directions.

Execution: Assume a standing position with your feet under your hips and hold a ten- to twenty-pound dumbbell in each hand. When you are ready, go into a slight crouch and leap up as high as possible. Once you are airborne, split your legs with one going forward and one going backward. Hold this position to land in the stride position. (See Fig. 7.5.) Immediately after landing, jump back up and scissor the legs again. Repeat in an alternating manner. The key to successful execution is to leap up as high as possible with full ankle-joint extension and straightening of the legs.

(a)   **(b)**   **(c)**

Figure 7.5   Split squat jump

5. *Explosive Knee Drive.* The explosive knee drive enables you to drive the trail (swing) leg forward as quickly as possible.

Execution: This exercise is done in basically the same manner as the knee-drive exercise for strength. The only difference is faster initial speed of execution and greater tension on the Active Cord (or weights on the cable). When you are ready, inhale and hold your breath as you start driving the thigh forward as quickly as possible. (See Fig. 7.6.) Do not drive your knee all the way up to the level position. The key is to have maximum tension when you begin the forward movement so that the movement stops when the leg is slightly in front of the body.

6. *Jump Out of a Squat.* This movement utilizes the built-up muscular tension in a holding position by exploding out of a stationary position. This exercise is very beneficial for improving reaction time.

Execution: Assume a half- to full-squat position. Your legs should have approximately a 145-degree angle in the knee joints, and your trunk should be inclined slightly forward. Hold the position for two to five seconds and then leap up as forcefully as possible. After landing, go into position and hold ready to repeat. (See Fig. 7.7.)

When working on reaction time have someone give you a signal to start. The signal should be auditory or visual and vary in intensity. For example, the command could be quiet, loud, or in between. When using visual signals, have a slight hand movement indicate a go, or use a full movement of the hand or other body part to signal start.

7. *Skip Jump (Power Skip).* This exercise is used to coordinate the leg pushoff with the knee drive.

Execution: Begin by taking a few steps and then push off the ground on one leg and drive the opposite knee upward at the same time. When you leave the ground the pushoff leg should be fully extended and the swing-leg knee drive should approach level. Upon landing on the swing leg, take a short skip and then jump, using the opposite leg for the knee drive. (See Fig. 7.8.) Distance and speed of forward movement are not important in this exercise; concentrate on maximum vertical height and ankle extension.

8. *Double-Leg Jump in Place.* This exercise promotes greater concentration on full ankle-joint extension and preparation for a good landing.

Execution: Assume a standing position with your feet directly under your hips. When ready, bend your legs slightly, swing your arms down and around, and leap up as high as possible with full extension of the legs. Make sure your legs are straight and toes are pointed. On touchdown, land close to the arch of the foot, i.e., on the ball and then heel almost simultaneously. (See Fig 7.9.) Execute the landing and take-

(a)

(b)

Figure 7.6 Explosive knee drive

(a)   **(b)**

Figure 7.7   Jump out of a squat

(a)   **(b)**   **(c)**

Figure 7.8   Skip jump

off as quickly as possible. It must be explosive! Prepare yourself mentally and physically for each landing and takeoff. If you are sufficiently strong, landing and takeoff can be done on the balls of the feet only. Be sure the foot is angled approximately 20 to 30 degrees on the landing.

9. Double-Leg Jump for Height and Distance.   When you have mastered the standing jump, begin the double-leg jump for height and some distance. This

exercise is used to direct your forces upward and slightly forward.

Execution: Execution is the same as in double-leg jump in place, except in the takeoff you incline your body forward slightly so that after you leap you will come down approximately twelve to eighteen inches in front of the takeoff spot. (See Fig. 7.10.)

10. Single-Leg Jump in Place.   This exercise improves your ability to land and take off on one leg. The key

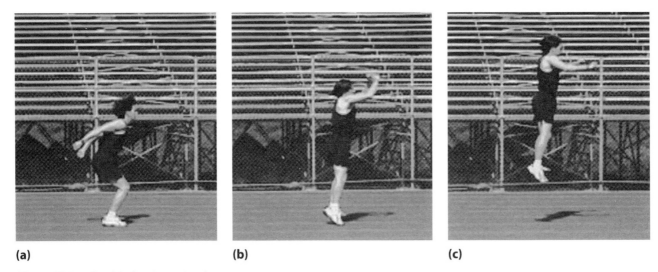

(a)   (b)   (c)

Figure 7.9   Double-leg jump in place

(a)   (b)

(c)   (d)

Figure 7.10   Double-leg jump for height and distance

to successful execution of this exercise is to leap up as high as possible in a vertical direction and execute the landing and takeoff as quickly as possible. You should master this exercise before doing single-leg jumps with forward movement.

Execution: Stand on one leg in a well-balanced position. When you are ready, swing your arms down and around and then up. As your arms come up, drive the swing-leg knee upward. As the arms and knee are driven upward, fully straighten the support leg and strongly extend the ankle joint to leap up as high as possible. Prepare for the landing mentally and physically and as soon as you make ground contact, cushion and withstand the forces to execute another quick jump upward. (See Fig. 7.11.)

11. Single-Leg Jump with Forward Movement. Single-leg jumps with forward movement are used to direct the forces upward and forward. These actions are especially important in basketball, football, and soccer.

Execution: Execute the same as the single-leg jump in place but direct the forces slightly forward on each jump. You should land approximately

(a)

(b)

(c)

(d)

Figure 7.11 Single-leg jump in place

twelve to eighteen inches in front of the initial take-off point. (See Fig. 7.12.)

12. Ankle Jump. Ankle jumps emphasize ankle-joint extension as needed in the pushoff.

Execution: Assume a standing position with your feet directly under your hips. Keep your legs slightly bent, and concentrate on jumping solely with ankle-joint extension. The height will not be great since it is necessary to eliminate knee-joint extension as much as possible. The range of motion in the knee joint should be no more than 10 to 15 degrees while the ankle joint goes through the full range of motion (about 60 to 80 degrees). Your toes should be pointed downward on every jump and your legs

should be straight. (See Fig. 7.13.) Use weights for increased resistance.

13. Double-Leg Jump for Distance Bounding. This exercise develops the ability to execute explosive takeoffs on both legs in an upward-forward direction. The key is to concentrate on both height and distance.

Execution: Execute as in the regular double-leg takeoff for height, except incline your body forward at approximately a 45-degree angle at takeoff. Be sure your legs are fully extended on takeoff. Upon landing, execute the next takeoff as quickly as possible. (See Fig. 7.14.) If you find yourself sinking too low and the jump takes too long to execute, cut down on the distance.

(a)

(b)

(c)

(d)

Figure 7.12 Single-leg jump with forward movement

(a)

(b)

Figure 7.13   Ankle jump

(a)

(b)

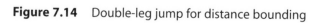

(c)

(d)

Figure 7.14   Double-leg jump for distance bounding

14. Medicine Ball Throw Backward. This exercise is used to get full extension of the body; develop more explosive legs; and give you the feel of a fully extended, slightly arched body as seen in a full running stride.

Execution: Stand holding a medicine ball in two hands below your waist. When you are ready, bend your knees slightly, incline your trunk, and go into a slight crouch. Then raise your body, leap off the ground, keep your arms straight and throw the ball over your head as high and as far back as possible. (See Fig. 7.15.) When first starting this exercise, get the feel of throwing the ball backward with only your arms and then gradually incorporate use of the legs and body. Also, begin with easy throws and gradually build up to full power.

15. Medicine Ball Throw Forward. This move develops the ability to direct explosive forces upward and slightly forward with resistance. It requires total body coordination.

Execution: Assume a standing position with your feet directly under your hips, holding a medicine ball in both hands below the waist. When you are ready, go into a slight crouch (squat) and then leap up and at the same time raise your arms to release the ball at the top of your jump. Be sure to keep your arms straight when releasing the ball and

fully extend the legs and ankle joints as you leave the ground. You should land approximately two to three feet in front of your takeoff point. (See Fig. 7.16.)

16. Leaping. This exercise is very beneficial in developing the ability to take a quick first step. When executed well, it improves simultaneous pushoff and knee drive, especially as needed in sprinting. It comes close to duplicating your position when airborne.

Execution: Take a few approach steps and then leap forward as far as possible, taking off on one leg. The swing leg should be bent at the knee and driven forward at the same time the pushoff takes place. Your body should remain as low as possible in the takeoff and flight phase, and your airborne position should be almost the same as in sprinting. As you prepare for landing, swing the forward leg down and back to once again push yourself forward as forcefully as possible. Be sure your trunk is erect and your body is well in front of the pushoff leg when ground contact is broken so that almost all the forces are directed horizontally. (See Fig. 7.17.)

Do not confuse this exercise with what some coaches call single-leg bounding. In bounding, the takeoff is more vertical and your body does not remain low to the ground.

(a)   (b)   (c)

Figure 7.15 Medicine ball throw backward

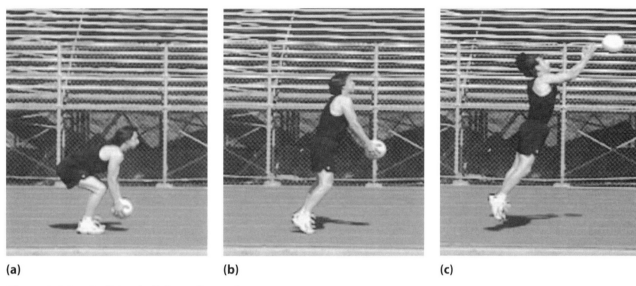

(a)　　　　　　　　　　　**(b)**　　　　　　　　　　　**(c)**

Figure 7.16　Medicine ball throw forward

(a)　　　　　　　　　　　**(b)**　　　　　　　　　　　**(c)**

Figure 7.17　Leaping

17. *Explosive Arm Drive with Rubber Tubing.* This exercise develops greater force and speed in driving the arm forward to synchronize with a powerful knee drive. It is especially important for sprinters.

Execution: Assume a standing position, holding the handle of the Active Cord in your hand slightly behind your body with your elbow slightly bent and to the rear. When you are ready, inhale and hold your breath as you drive your arm forward and bend the elbow to a 90-degree angle. Drive the arm forward until the upper arm is alongside the body and your hand is approximately shoulder high. Straighten your arm and return to the initial position under control, and exhale. Then get ready to repeat. (See Fig. 7.18.)

General Recommendations for Jumping

1. When first starting speed-strength training, keep the intensity low. To increase intensity, gradually increase the height of your jumps or increase the amount of resistance used.

(a)   (b)   (c)

Figure 7.18   Explosive arm drive using rubber tubing

2. Begin with double-leg jumps and then move on to single-leg jumps.

3. Start with vertical jumping and later incorporate horizontal jumping.

4. Gradually increase jumping repetitions in the initial stages of training. As you move into the specialized training period increase the intensity (height) of jumping and decrease repetitions. (This is analogous to what you do in the progression of changes in weight training.)

5. When you first start jump training, jump on surfaces that are neither too hard nor too soft. The key is that they be somewhat resilient, for example, gymnastic and wrestling mats, gym floors, a grassy field, etc. Never do jump training on concrete.

6. For strengthening the joints, especially the ankle joint, and to prevent injuries, also do some barefoot running and easy jumping.

7. Always execute lead-up, or preparatory, jumps before doing true full-intensity plyometric jumps.

8. When doing lead-up, or preparatory, jumps, do not execute the jumps maximally, but maintain good jump technique. When doing easy jumps such as rope skipping, do anywhere from ten to twenty jumps in a row. Gauge the amount of such lead-up jumps on how you feel and how long it takes for you to get ready for maximal (high-intensity) jumping.

9. When doing true plyometric (speed-strength) jumps, do no more than ten in a row. Be sure you have adequate rest between sets.

10. Always land on both feet except when doing single-leg jumps. When you land on one foot, you have twice the amount of force in comparison to landing on both feet.

11. In the early stages of training, do only two to three exercises and execute one set.

12. As you develop the ability to do jump exercises more easily and effectively, add more exercises and sets to the program.

13. In general, do no more than six to ten explosive jump exercises in a row, especially when done for two to three sets each.

14. Be sure you begin jump and plyometric exercises after an adequate warm-up and after you have completed the active stretches. Strength training for the legs can follow jump training.

CHAPTER

8

Running Barefoot

When you are asked about running and what is involved, you most likely will focus on the role of the legs and arms. Rarely do runners think of the role of the feet, even though feet are involved in every step and have a very important function in the landing, support phase, and pushoff. Many runners believe shoes take care of the feet.

When foot problems are discussed, they are usually related to topics such as blisters, bunions, ingrown toenails, and sweating. When other foot problems, such as oversupination and overpronation occur, immediate thought goes to getting running shoes (or orthotics) to correct these problems. Rarely is attention given to strengthening and improving the functions of the foot and ankle. Instead of relying on the natural and very effective functions of the foot, we have come to rely on artificial support structures such as running shoes, orthotics, and insoles.

This does not mean that support equipment does not play an important role. It does. What runners often ignore is whether the equipment interferes with or prevents the proper functioning of the foot in running. For example, if your shoe has a built-up firm arch, it will not allow the foot's arch

to compress and return to its original shape during landing and takeoff. As a result, if the shoe is used over a long period of time, the arch muscles, tendons, and ligaments get weaker and lose their ability to handle the landing forces and produce additional force in the pushoff. Eventually the muscles may atrophy, creating a weaker foot that must rely on more artificial support structures to maintain foot integrity.

Running Shoes

According to the advertisements, running shoes are well constructed and it is now possible to find a shoe to "fix" almost all problems encountered by runners. There are shoes that prevent pronation or supination, and if you are a heel hitter there are shoes to cushion each touchdown. Some shoes provide lateral support while others have arch support. From a technology standpoint, these shoes may be extremely valuable in treating certain foot problems. But it is important to determine if all these supports are needed by an individual who has a well-functioning, normal foot. Have modern-day runners become invalids who now require such foot support? If yes, I often wonder how man survived running before the advent of shoes.

Many foot studies have been done in nations where people walk and run barefoot (the Philippines, Central Africa, Belgium, the Congo, Solomon Islands, China, India, and Vietnam). They have concluded that the unshod human foot is characterized by excellent mobility (especially of the forefoot); thickening of the plantar skin; alignment of the phalanges with the metatarsals that causes the toes to spread; variability in arch height; and, in general, strong, injury-free, well-functioning feet.

These results are not surprising since the foot is especially well constructed from a structural and mechanical standpoint to handle most running problems. The foot support structures, consisting of the bones, ligaments, tendons, and muscles, are extremely effective in maintaining normal foot posture and in withstanding various forces that act on the foot in running. When these natural support structures are not used, as occurs when various running shoes are worn, the muscles, tendons, and ligaments become weaker.

Once the natural foot structures are weakened, it becomes necessary to rely on external support structures (such as running shoes) to take over the normal functions of the foot. But the support given by various shoes does not match that given by a well-functioning foot, nor is the support functional. For example, high-top shoes supposedly give lateral support to the ankle. But the only way they can do this is to have the laces tied snugly all the way to the top. This severely limits the range of motion in the ankle, which in turn interferes with the ability to walk and run. Look closely at basketball players who wear high-tops and you will see that they are very loose fitting around the ankle. This shoe looseness allows players to run and jump as needed in the game, but without the lateral support.

Some running-shoe studies indicate that running shoes are the cause of many running injuries. This makes sense for two important reasons: (1) the shoes allow you to run incorrectly by landing on the heel, which creates high braking forces, and (2) the shoes do not allow the support structures to function as needed in the running stride.

Running shoes may also be responsible for other problems. For example, I recently worked with a young female runner who had severe ankle and knee problems. After videotaping her, I saw no major discrepancies in technique that could be causing the problem. I then videotaped the foot action very carefully. When she ran wearing running shoes it was possible to see foot overpronation very clearly. I then had her run barefoot, and to our surprise, there was no excessive overpronation. The foot remained in perfect alignment with the shin during landing and takeoff. The overpronation was caused by the shoes, which in turn caused the ankle and knee problems. Once we changed shoes, the problems were alleviated.

A recent study by physical therapists Bruce Wilk and William Gutierrez found that 30 to 50 percent of new running shoes have defects that can lead to running problems. In addition, there was no difference in higher priced shoes. This study was published in the Winter 2000 issue of *The American Medical Athletic Association Journal* (volume 14, no. 1).

Role of the Tendons and Ligaments

Instead of relying on external shoe support, you should strengthen the foot support structures to improve your running and regain a normal well-functioning foot. One very simple and effective way of doing this is to walk and run barefoot. When you are barefoot, your support structures go into action to support your body weight and the forces encountered, and most important, to make walking and running more effective and efficient. For example, on touchdown in running, the foot ligaments and tendons immediately go into action to cushion the landing by absorbing some of the landing forces. They also accumulate or withstand the landing forces in the forced stretch of tendons, especially in the foot arch.

Much of the muscle activity in running is associated with stretching and tensing the tendons to store elastic energy for successive cycles of movement. Tensing the tendons is achieved with very little change in the length of the muscle fibers that gives you greater economy of energy expenditure.

The ability to store elastic energy depends on the velocity of the stretching, the magnitude of the stretch, and the duration of the transition between termination of the eccentric and initiation of the concentric phases of movement. The delay between these two phases should be minimal or the stored elastic energy will be rapidly dissipated. In essence, the human foot behaves like a spring, capable of storing and returning up to 70 percent of the energy that goes into it. Running shoes do not even come close to this figure!

In a well-functioning foot there is very little compression, which in turn equates to greater force. The more compression, the more absorption takes place. But for return of energy there should only be a slight depression and then a quick return. To see this in the human foot, look at Fig. 3.36 in Chapter 3. In frame *b* you can see the foot arch as it prepares for landing. In frame *c*, as the foot makes contact, you can see some compression of the dome, and in *d* even more compression of the dome. In *e*, as the heel begins to leave the ground, you can see the arch becoming greater, especially in frame *f* and thereafter. These figures show a good return of energy.

The Achilles tendon is very powerful and plays a major role in return of energy in running. This tendon can withstand tremendous landing forces and give them back in the pushoff, which makes running very economical and is the basis for increased speed. During the takeoff in sprinting, external energy increases by 340 joules (J). The knee-joint muscles do only 31J of work, and the plantar flexors do 192J—or more than six times as much. Therefore, the main driving link in running with maximum sustained speed is the foot!

Much has been written about the need to absorb the landing forces to prevent injury. This is only partially true, especially when the very efficient functions of the foot ligaments, tendons, and muscles are taken into consideration. Some absorption is needed on immediate touchdown, but if all the forces were absorbed, the muscles and support structures would have to do a tremendous amount of extra work to create the energy needed for support and for the pushoff in each running stride. This would be very inefficient.

In effective long-distance running, touchdown occurs on mid-foot, so that the arch of the foot immediately goes into action to absorb some forces but withstand most. The arch flattens somewhat and then reassumes its dome shape to give back energy during the pushoff and to then relax in its normal shape. The depression and expansion of the arch is a key feature of a well-functioning foot and is indicative of the muscle-tendon resiliency. When you land on the heel, however, the support structures cannot go into action to absorb and withstand the forces.

In sprinting, touchdown occurs on the ball of the foot, followed immediately by the heel or close to mid-foot. With such landings, the arch of the foot immediately goes into action to absorb some of the forces as the arch dome depresses. In the process the muscles, ligaments, and tendons tense up to withstand the forces and store them to give back in the pushoff when the foot arch reassumes its dome shape.

The more the support structures can withstand and give back this energy in the depression and return to the normal arch dome, the greater the running efficiency. Such changes in shape show muscle-tendon resiliency and are indicative of how the foot functions to prevent injury on the landing and to economize on energy in the takeoff. Landing on the heel, however, does not allow the support structures to function in their normal manner to absorb, withstand, and give back most of the landing forces.

Much has been written about the type of foot arch you may possess. According to some individuals, an extremely high arch is detrimental as is a too-low arch or flat foot. However, the size of the arch is not as important as what happens to the arch in running. The key to a well-functioning arch is whether it is capable of being compressed and returning to normal as quickly as possible. If your foot arch becomes compressed and does not quickly return to its dome shape, then it is not functioning very well. In addition to the arch being compressed, it is important to note that the toes also should spread out to provide a larger base during the support phase. As a result, the big toe is placed in a position where it is capable of flexing on the pushoff to contribute even more force.

Barefoot Running

There is much scientific and empirical evidence to show the value of barefoot running. For example, the Tarahumara Indians of Mexico, who are famous for running 200 miles over hilly, rocky terrain at high altitudes while wearing sandals made of rubber tires and leather thongs, rarely experience foot or leg problems. As mentioned earlier, people who go barefoot do not experience the foot problems seen in industrialized nations where shoes are worn almost all the time. Sadly, wearing shoes has come to symbolize affluence and is considered a sign of being civilized. Can you imagine seeing someone in the city walking barefoot and not thinking that individual was uncouth? Yet walking and running barefoot (where conditions permit) are some of the best things we can do for our feet.

In barefoot running, you are forced to execute good technique by landing on the mid-foot. If you are a heel hitter, you can do this with well-cushioned heels in running shoes, but landing on your heel while running barefoot on a solid surface would hurt so much you would not be able to do it! This shows that landing on the heel is not a normal way to run. In every foot plant, you should bring into play the foot support structures, not only for safety but for efficiency. Thus, in barefoot running you can learn better technique.

As you learn to run more effectively, you strengthen the foot support structures, which then enable you to run longer and farther, safer and more efficiently. As the foot (and leg) support structures get stronger, fewer injuries are experienced and running becomes easier and more comfortable. In essence, you can enhance your running performance with proper running technique and by strengthening the support structures so that they can function well.

Many, if not most, running injuries stem from the foot allowing excessive forces to travel up the body to cause injury to the knee, hip, or lower back. These negative forces are most often caused by poor technique and inefficient running shoes. Some studies show that the more money runners spend on their shoes, the greater the number of injuries they incur! In my work with runners, I have found similar results. This is why I have always recommended that runners buy the cheapest shoes possible as long as they have a good fit and feel comfortable. Good running technique is a prerequisite. The shoes then serve to protect the feet against ground objects.

Getting Started Running Barefoot

When starting to run barefoot, it is important that you build up gradually so you do not overstress the plantar fascia or the ligaments and tendons of the foot, as well as the Achilles tendon. Begin by walking barefoot every opportunity you can. As you become accustomed to walking barefoot, start easy jogging on the balls of the feet, gradually moving into a full stride.

The key to barefoot running is to become familiar with landing close to the arch of the foot (mid-foot). In long-distance running, the foot makes contact slightly in front of the body on the ball of the foot, followed immediately by the heel, or on mid-foot. You can also land on the heel of the foot close to the arch, followed immediately by the ball of the foot. In no case should you land on the heel with the foot up at approximately a 30- to 45-degree angle. This is highly dangerous. Landing close to the arch so that the arch of the foot can immediately go into action to absorb and withstand the landing forces is the key to safe and effective running. There should be some compression and then a return to the original dome shape of the foot so that you experience the feeling of resiliency and springiness on each stride.

Good landing technique appears to be the major adaptation made by barefoot runners. Because running-related injuries are rare, it indicates that humans adapted to barefoot running by experiencing lower impact forces than an unadapted foot. When runners unaccustomed to barefoot running run barefoot, they experience impact on landing that is no higher than when shod, and in some cases is lower because of the foot actions.

Your feet should be capable of absorbing and withstanding impact forces, but you have to stimulate that capability by going barefoot. When the arch compresses and returns to its dome shape, the muscles spanning the arch become more conditioned, more flexible, and eventually more impervious to impact.

Also beneficial when getting started is to do some exercises to strengthen the plantar structures, especially the arch of the foot. Do exercises such as picking up marbles with the toes, and walking or jogging on the balls of the feet. Ankle adduction exercises are also important for maintaining the foot arch. Build up gradually so your feet get accustomed to the work and become stronger. Because you've been wearing shoes with so much "support," your foot structures have weakened considerably. It will take time for them to get sufficiently strong to withstand the forces encountered in running.

Systematic training in barefoot walking and running on uneven ground has a reflex reaction bringing about multiple muscle contractions to uphold the arch of the foot and muscles of the plantar surface, including the flexors of the toes. This leads to strengthening the toe flexors together with the ligaments and tendons. Thus, walking and running barefoot can be used as prophylactic measures and for rehabilitating flat-footedness.

People who develop epidermophytosis rarely walk barefoot. As a result, they have a very thin epidermal layer of the sole of the foot and the needed skin between the toes. Since this problem is not seen in barefoot walkers, dermatologists, as a means of preventing and even curing epidermophytosis, recommend more frequent walking without shoes. They also note that walking and running barefoot are effective means of preventing formation of corns, intertrigo, and other disabilities, and decrease sweating of the feet.

Other Benefits

In the last few years, fitness leaders have recommended more running. To make this recommendation even more effective, it should include running barefoot. Think of running barefoot as a therapeutic, prophylactic measure and as a way to maintain a well-functioning foot.

Many people get involved in running mainly to avoid heart attacks and other cardiovascular problems. This is great to see, but there are still other objectives that are very important. According to some doctors, one is the prevention of illnesses. The stimulating activity of many defense mechanisms, which protect individuals against colds and flu, simultaneously increase and strengthen health when running barefoot. Reflexes arising from activity on the skin surface are natural factors, as are sunshine, air, and water, which act through the central nervous system to activate many important physiological functions. These functions have a positive effect on the nervous, cardiovascular, and respiratory systems, and improve the exchange of various products.

Reaching greater levels of fitness requires working out and using effective new forms and methods of physical activity that can be easily incorporated into one's lifestyle. One reason barefoot walking and running are so important is that in today's society many activities formerly done barefoot are now done in shoes, and everyone must have a particular shoe in order to do each activity. Barefoot walking and running are often considered signs of an uncivilized or uncultured people.

After waking up in the morning, the first thing most people do is put on slippers before going to the bathroom or kitchen. They wear slippers before going to bed, and during the day they wear shoes from morning to night. This occurs all day, throughout their lifetimes. Youngsters who strive hard to run, jump, and play barefoot are forced to put on shoes so they don't catch cold, their feet won't be "deformed," and to look "in style."

Running barefoot also has great influence on many body functions through the tactile sensors, a function of the skin on the sole of the foot. There are many mechanoreceptors that have different types of tactile sense from very fine to high levels of pain. For every square centimeter of skin, there are on average up to 200 mechanoreceptors, and on the sole of the foot, there are even more. The reason for this probably lies in the fact that in the evolution of humankind there was a gradual buildup of the sensors on the feet so we could feel and distinguish against the ground. These are properties humans still possess and that can be made more functional.

Troubleshooting: Special Exercises to Resolve Common Problems

You are now armed with the knowledge of what constitutes effective running and how you can improve and enhance your running. However, very often the solution to correcting your flaws may not always be obvious. You may still have difficulty executing the key actions and making changes to learn the new technique. Practicing more will not work if you do not have the ability to execute the exact movements needed.

I recently worked with one of the top long-distance runners in Southern California. His technique had many positive aspects but his touchdown was very passive, occurred too far in front of the body, and was on the heel followed immediately by the whole foot. He had some pawback action but it was extremely weak. Although he understood what had to be done, he had difficulty executing the movement and making his foot plant active.

When I questioned him about the pawback movement, he responded that he consciously thought he was bringing the leg back to make ground contact. It was not until I gave him an exercise—the straight-leg pullback—to develop the feel of pulling the leg down and back in an active manner, that he mastered the ability to execute this action. As he developed the necessary hamstring strength and the feel of executing this action, he was able to incorporate it into his technique. But without first developing the muscular feel, he was unable to make the necessary change.

When doing exercises to correct common problems, it is important that you do the exercises for two different effects. For example, to develop the feel of the movement it is not necessary to use a great amount of weight. The key here is to do more repetitions so you learn the neuromuscular feel of the action. This sometimes is sufficient to correct the problem. If, however, the problem is lack of muscle, you must exercise for strength. Here you must have ample resistance and a sufficient number of repetitions to develop not only the feel, but also the strength and endurance needed to execute the movement effectively.

To assist in improving your running, I have identified some common running flaws and developed solutions employing special exercises. As you master the special exercises, you will develop the strength, flexibility, and muscular feel for the movement, allowing you to duplicate the movement in your running stride and execute it well. You will feel the action when you incorporate it into other movements that are already strongly ingrained. In this way, the specialized exercises can bring your weak points up to par with your strong points. (These exercises are described in detail in Chapters 5–7.)

Problem 1: The swing-leg knee does not rise sufficiently during the drive phase.

The main reason this occurs is that the forward knee drive is not sufficiently forceful and does not move in a horizontal direction. The exact height of the thigh is determined by how powerfully the thigh is driven forward. It is a resultant position determined by your speed of running, not one you actively try to achieve. For example, look at Figs. 3.40a and 3.40j. The runner has a very forceful pushoff but the thigh does not rise up to the height that it should in relation to the force of the pushoff. This shows that he is not concentrating on pulling the thigh through, which is also seen in Figs. 3.40f and 3.40o. When he is in the support phase the swing leg is still far behind.

Solution: Forward knee drive, with rubber tubing, and lunge.

When doing the forward knee drive, be sure your leg is as far behind your body as it is in the actual running stride and that the movement is executed forcefully. For example, the swing-leg thigh should be at least 45 degrees behind the erect trunk position when beginning the knee drive. In sprinting it may be more. Also, if the leg is not sufficiently behind the body, it indicates lack of flexibility in the hip joint, which can be corrected by doing the lunge exercise.

Problem 2: Touchdown on the heel, with the sole of the foot angled up.

The heel hit is a strong blocking and braking action that slows you down on each footstep, even if it is for only a fraction of a second. It also leads to too much vertical displacement in the pushoff, which is not economical and directs your forces ineffectively. And the amount of force developed in mild heel hitting is not as great as when the sole of the

foot is angled up approximately 45 degrees, an extreme most often seen in lower-level runners.

Solution: Straight-leg pulldown.

To eliminate the heel hit, it is necessary to bring the straight leg down and back (execute pawback) so touchdown occurs more on the whole foot. Do not simply bend the knee to land on mid-foot as more runners are beginning to do. This still creates braking forces because of the forward-of-the-body position on touchdown. To develop the feel and muscle strength involved in this action, you should do the straight-leg pullback with touchdown on the ball of the foot or mid-foot.

Problem 3: Too much up-and-down motion.

The more your center of gravity is moved up and down in each running stride, the less efficient your run. Not only does vertical movement require more energy, but it slows you down and brings on early fatigue. For example, look at Fig. 3.28e. The runner is running at an 800-meter pace, which is closer to a sprint, yet the angle of knee bend is similar to that of a marathon runner. Also Figs. 3.31b and 3.31k show excessive knee bend, especially since the body weight has still not come fully over the leg. In this case the excessive knee bend may not be due to lack of muscle strength but a technique change to prevent the heel hit.

Solution: Squat and pawback.

There are two main reasons for too much up-and-down motion during the support phase. Very often it is due to lack of sufficient eccentric and isometric strength of the quadriceps muscle of the support leg. To strengthen this muscle, you should do the squat. Execute very slowly with some stops on the down phase for greater eccentric and isometric strength increases. Excessive up-and-down motion may also be due to not executing the pawback action (which creates the heel hit). The more your foot lands in front of your body, the longer it takes for your body to move over the support leg so that, when pushoff occurs, it drives your body upward instead of forward. Thus it is necessary to do the pawback exercise.

Problem 4: Excessively high leg recovery (as though you are trying to kick your butt).

For maximum economy in long-distance running, it is important that the shin be approximately level (or slightly above level) as the thigh is driven forward. Raising the shin higher so the heel comes close to the buttocks when the thigh is almost vertical is wasted energy and slows down forward leg movement. In sprinting, the heel comes close to the buttocks but with the knee well in front of the body. If the heel is close to the buttocks when the knee is pointed straight down, it is wasted action that slows you down.

For example, if you look at Figs. 3.29, 3.35, 3.37, and 3.40, you will see that each of these long-distance runners has an excessively high recovery leg. It is as if the runners were trying to kick themselves in the buttocks. This also indicates that they are not relaxing the leg after the pushoff to economize on energy. They are actively working the hamstring muscles instead of allowing them to relax somewhat.

Solution: Explosive knee drive with rubber tubing.

To correct an excessively high leg-recovery position in the flight phase it is important to emphasize a strong thigh drive in the pushoff, and at the same time, relax the leg muscles, especially the hamstrings. The shin will rise to approximately the level position because of the rearward forces developed in the pushoff, and should remain there as you pull the thigh through. Actively contracting the hamstrings will raise the foot—an undesirable action. The knee-drive exercise with rubber tubing emphasizes the forward drive with the shin level to the ground. This exercise will also correct this flaw in sprinting.

Problem 5: Excessive forward lean of the trunk.

A forward lean is needed only when accelerating. When in full stride, regardless of whether you are a long-distance runner or sprinter, your trunk should be erect. A 1- to 5-degree angle of lean is acceptable but no lean is most effective. If you look at Figs. 3.29 through 3.35 you will see that all the runners are basically erect. There is a slight crouch during the support phase but during the pushoff and flight the trunk is erect.

If you examine Fig. 9.1, however, you will see an excessive forward lean by the sprinter. The lean may be explained partially by his being an outstanding football player, but more to his belief that he should be leaning forward at all times. This was hammered into him by his coaches. Having a constant forward lean inhibits thigh action and the ability to reach out and execute a strong pawback.

Solution: Back raise, glute-ham-gastroc raise, and lunge.

The forward lean in many runners is usually due to weak lower-back and hip-extensor muscles or tight hip-joint flexor muscles. Back raises and the glute-ham-gastroc raise (or hip extension) strengthen these muscles. If excessive forward lean is due to overly tight hip-flexor muscles, you should do the lunge, to actively stretch these muscles.

Problem 6: Full extension (straightening) of the pushoff leg.

When you fully extend the pushoff leg, you begin to leap rather than maintaining a running pattern. This disrupts your normal cadence and uses more energy by strongly contracting the quadriceps muscles to straighten the leg. It is more effective to rely on the resilient properties of the lower-leg tendons and muscles as used in ankle extension, the main pushoff action, while keeping the pushoff leg slightly bent in the knee.

For example, if you look at Figs. 3.4, 3.29e, 3.33c, 3.35f, and 3.40j, you can see a straight leg in the pushoff. To see the bent leg that is a more effective technique, see Figs. 3.1d, 3.32d, 3.34h and i, 3.37d, and 3.41d. Note that even though the amount of leg extension is not great it still saps energy and interferes with a smooth running pattern. Most of the leg extension occurs when the upper body moves well in front of the pushoff leg.

Solution: Ankle jump or explosive heel raises.

By focusing on full ankle-joint extension in the pushoff you take attention away from the knee, which should remain stabilized in a slightly bent

(a)   (b)   (c)   (d)

(e)   (f)   (g)

Figure 9.1   Steve Metz

position. To develop the feel for this action do explosive heel raises, with a hold in the top position, and ankle jumps.

Problem 7: A passive foot strike.

It is not uncommon in some runners, especially long-distance runners, to see the swing leg come forward and the shin swing out to straighten the leg, remaining in this position until contact with the ground. Holding the leg in front until touchdown takes valuable time, which decreases your running speed. In addition, by maintaining your leg in front, you invariably land on the heel, which also slows you and leads to other problems.

Solution: The pullback (pawback).

To correct a passive foot strike, you should concentrate on whipping the leg back immediately as full leg

extension takes place. In other words, after you drive the knee forward and swing the shin out, quickly bring the straight leg down and back. Do not hold the leg out in front. You can get the feel of a one-motion forward swing out followed by a pullback when doing the leg pullback exercise with rubber tubing.

You may also want to do the circling or wheeling drill. In a standing position raise the knee, reach out with the foot until the leg is straight and then drive the straight leg down and back. Make direction changes smoothly so that when viewed from the side the foot makes a circle. Concentrate on the latter part of the movement, the straightening and pulling-down phase.

Problem 8: Insufficient separation between the thighs during and immediately after the pushoff.

In sprinting, it should be possible to see approximately a 150- to 165-degree separation between the thighs, while in long-distance running separation is closer to 90 degrees. Insufficient separation can be due to lack of flexibility of the hip-joint muscles, insufficient force in the forward knee drive, or a more vertical pushoff. For example, in Fig. 3.29d, directly after the pushoff and in the flight phase there is insufficient separation between the sprinter's thighs. He has a strong knee drive seen by the slightly forward position of the swing-leg thigh when the support leg is in contact with the ground and does not have a strong vertical component. Thus the problem is insufficient range of motion in the hip joint.

In Figs. 3.35k and 3.35t, the foot is in full support on the ground and the swing leg is still trailing behind. This indicates a weak knee drive, mainly because of the extremely high recovery for a marathon distance pace. If there is a weak pullback action, the pushoff will occur early, which drives the body upward more than necessary. For example, in Figs. 3.31c and 3.37b, the heel is already off the ground. This indicates the beginning of the pushoff. But with a stronger pullback action, when the foot makes contact with the ground the upper body will move in front more.

Solution: Lunge, forward knee drive, and pawback.

The solution for insufficient hip-joint range of motion is to do the lunge active stretch to increase flexibility of the hip-flexor muscles. To improve the knee drive to prevent high recovery, do the forward knee-drive exercise in a more explosive manner with rubber tubing. To work on the pullback action, do the straight-leg pullback exercise.

Problem 9: The swing leg is still behind the body during full support.

In efficient running, the swing-leg thigh should be alongside the support-leg thigh, so that when viewed from the side you should only see one thigh. When the swing leg is still behind the body, it means you are not driving it forward with sufficient force, or you have an excessively high leg recovery. For example, if you look at Figs. 3.26, 3.28e, 3.31k, and 3.40o, you can see the leg in full support with the swing leg still

behind the support leg. You will notice also that in Figs. 3.28, 3.35, and 3.40, the recovery is also too high. Thus, correcting one or both of these problems may serve as an effective solution.

Solution: Forward knee drive, relaxing the hamstrings.

Concentrate on developing a powerful forward knee drive to bring the swing-leg thigh in line with the support thigh when there is full contact with the ground. This is also a very important force-producing action.

Problem 10: Keeping the arms flexed in sprinting.

Maintaining a 90-degree angle in the elbow joint is needed for economy in long-distance running. In sprinting, however, the legs work in synchronization with the arms. Thus when the leg is in full support, the arm should be straightened to slow its movement and at the same time create more ground-reaction forces that can be given back in the pushoff. In the photos in Chapter 3 you will note that sprinters (and even some long-distance runners) do not keep their arms flexed at a 90-degree angle. You will find this true of all good sprinters or other runners who run fast or sprint at the end of a race.

Solution: Triceps extension and lat pulldown.

To develop the ability to straighten and extend the arm as you go into the support phase, you should do elbow and shoulder-joint extension exercises.

Problem 11: Inability to maintain a 90-degree or less angle in the elbow joint in long-distance running.

Runners who open up the elbow in long-distance running have to expend greater energy in bringing the forearm back up to a 90-degree or less angle when bringing it forward. This becomes costly in terms of energy and should be avoided. However, when running faster than a marathon pace—for example, a 5K—or when speeding up at the end of the race, it is advantageous to straighten the arm somewhat as the foot is coming into contact with the ground.

Solution: Hold a 90-degree elbow-joint angle with a dumbbell in your hands.

In order to maintain the 90-degree angle in the elbow you must have adequate levels of isometric strength in the elbow flexors. To enhance your isometric strength, hold your elbows at a 90-degree angle with a dumbbell in your hands for greater resistance. Then move your arms forward and back in the running motion without opening up the elbow as the arm moves to the rear. You must get the feel of moving your upper arm from the shoulder.

Problem 12: Excessive shoulder rotation.

It is not uncommon to find runners rotating their shoulders to counteract rotation of the hips during each stride. However, the more the shoulders rotate, the greater the sideward-motion forces, which detract from the force needed to propel you directly forward as quickly and forcefully as possible. This usually indicates weak abdominal-rotational muscles or weak driving of the arms forward and backward.

For example, look at Figs. 3.31q–t, 3.35o, and 3.38d–g to see excessive shoulder rotation especially when compared to the position of the hips. In Fig. 3.35 you can see an extreme backward drive of the elbow, which compounds the shoulder rotation.

Solution: Reverse trunk twist and bent-arm forward raise.

Most important in preventing excessive shoulder rotation is to strengthen the abdominal-rotational muscles. When these muscles are strong, they stabilize the hips and shoulders to minimize rotation. In addition, the bent-arm forward raise improves arm action.

Problem 13: Leg is extended toward the ground during leg-straightening actions (shin swinging forward to make ground contact).

Some runners have an effective knee drive in which the knee rises to a sufficient height in front of the body. After the thigh reaches its uppermost position and as the shin swings out, instead of the thigh remaining raised, it drops so that the foot makes contact with the ground very quickly. In essence, as the shin swings forward, the leg is driven downward in a straightening action followed immediately by ground contact.

Once the leg is fully extended there is hardly any time to drive it back. The key is to maintain the thigh in basically the same position as the shin whips out and then to drive the straight leg down and back. This can also alleviate a passive foot strike, heel hit, and other problems.

Solution: The circling or wheeling exercise described in the solution to Problem 7.

Most runners seem to respond best to concentrating on maintaining the thigh up as they swing the leg out and then down. In essence, they must learn to drive the thigh forward and then reach out with the foot in front before driving the leg down and back. This means it is necessary to whip the shin forward somewhat faster in addition to holding the thigh upward, and then to bring in the pawback action.

Problem 14: Difficulty increasing stride length (when it is obviously not at the optimal amount).

Stride length is related to the three key force-producing actions in running: full ankle-joint extension in the pushoff, a powerful forward knee drive, and a powerful pawback action. Thus it is necessary to check which is at fault and do the exercises specific to that action. Or, you may have to enhance all three actions.

Solution: Heel raise, explosive heel raise, straight-leg pullback with rubber tubing, and the forward knee drive with rubber tubing.

To improve ankle-joint extension, do the heel raise for strength and the explosive heel raise through the full range of motion. Be sure to hold the top position for one to two seconds before repeating to get the feel of full extension. To improve the pawback action, do the straight-leg pullback with rubber tubing, and to improve the forward knee drive, do the explosive knee-drive exercise with rubber tubing.

Problem 15: Inadequate stride frequency.

In general, stride frequency depends on the explosiveness of the muscular contractions in the three major force-producing actions. By doing more explosive exercises for these actions you will improve stride length and stride frequency. Of the three actions to improve stride frequency, most important is the ankle-joint extension. In essence, the less time your foot is in contact with the ground, the greater your stride frequency (all other factors remaining the same). In addition, you must have adequate leg-muscle strength to prevent excessive lowering of the body during the support phase, which also takes up a tremendous amount of time.

Solution: Jump and plyometric exercises.

Jump and plyometric-type exercises are most effective for decreasing ground-contact time. These include single- and double-leg jumps, squat jumps, and stride jumps. The squat is important if you have too much body lowering during the support phase.

Problem 16: Not dorsi flexing the foot during swing out of the shin.

Limited dorsi flexion—raising the toe toward the shin—appears to be more of a problem with low-level runners. Better runners have this action, although in many of them it can be improved.

Solution: Toe raises with rubber tubing or on the Tib Exerciser.

I have found that in most cases the dorsi flexing problem is due to insufficient strength of the shin muscles, mainly the tibialis anterior shin muscle. By strengthening this muscle and being conscious of this action, runners become more capable of incorporating it into the run. This is especially true if they recognize the feel of raising the front of the foot when they do the exercise.

Problem 17: Moving the hand up and down rather than swinging the arm from the shoulder in synchronization with the leg action.

In some runners you can see that the elbow remains in place and the hand moves up and down in synchronization with the leg action. However, without swinging the arm forward and backward it is difficult to get full coordination between the arm and leg movements, which limits the range of motion in the hip joint. To be able to run with a full range of motion in the hips, it is important that you increase the range of motion of the arm in the shoulder joint. Once the arm moves forward and back, it is possible to incorporate opening the arm on the down phase and flexing it on the up phase to make the run more efficient, especially in sprinting.

Solution: Driving the arm forward, and swinging the arm forward and back.

The key action is pulling the elbow back and up and then bringing the arm forward until the elbow is alongside the body or slightly in front. Do not swing the elbow far in front of the body. This is wasted motion. Note that the further you bring the elbow in front, the higher your hand will rise so that, instead of your forces going forward, they are going upward. Also keep in mind that the elbow is not driven all the way back. It is lifted to the rear after the arm is either pulled down or swung back somewhat, as in long-distance running.

Problem 18: Insufficient ankle-joint extension.

Almost all runners use some ankle-joint extension in the pushoff. To be most effective, however, it is important to maximize the amount of ankle-joint extension. This is especially important for sprinters. For example, if you look at Fig. 3.1d you can see that ankle extension takes place, but between 3.1d and 3.1e the full ankle-joint extension that is needed in an 800-meter run does not occur.

Solution: Seated ankle-joint extension and explosive heel raise, with a hold after rising up.

When correcting a deficiency such as incomplete ankle-joint extension, it is first necessary to determine if the problem is due to inadequate flexibility or to lack of strength or explosive strength to enable the foot to go through the full range of motion. To improve ankle-joint flexibility, you should do the seated ankle-joint extension. To work on ensuring a full range of motion, it is important to do the ankle-extension exercise for strength with a hold at the top, or more specifically, the explosive heel raise with a hold at the end.

Problem 19: A strained face.

A strained face is usually indicative of excessive tightness in the body, especially the upper body. This inhibits fluid motion of the arms and legs, which detracts greatly from your running speed and efficiency.

Solution: Smile.

While in your running stride, smile to see if there is any change in your total body feeling. If you are tight, you will notice immediately how complete relaxation flows through your body when you smile. Do this every so often during the run to check on tightness and to learn the feeling of relaxing while maintaining your speed.

CHAPTER 10

Nutrition for Optimal Running

If you would like to be a great runner, you must give your body the right fuel. Your diet must satisfy your taste buds as well as your muscles, and there is a way of eating that will enhance your running and health. The only "diet" you should be on is the one you can stay on and enjoy for life. In essence, your eating habits must be part of your lifestyle.

Eating to Be Better

Engaging in an exercise or running program without the right diet is like trying to run your car without sufficient fuel or oil. Sooner or later the car is going to break down, or at best, just plain run out of gas. Think of food not as an enemy, but as a very important ally. Why? Because of a simple phenomenon known as supercompensation, which occurs in response to what is known as the training effect.

If you run more than you are accustomed, your body experiences a greater workload. As a result, you deplete the body's energy supplies in order to get the work accomplished. After the work is done, recovery begins to take place and some of the energy stores are

replaced quickly so that you have enough energy to continue doing various tasks during the day. The main recovery phase, however, takes place when you are sleeping. This is when the body goes to work to repair any damage that was done to the muscles and to restructure the muscles and support structures in response to the running (or training exercises) done. Glycogen stores are replenished, which brings energy levels back up, and many other functions take place to return your body to a stable state.

However, the body does not only compensate for what you have done or replace your original energy supply. Because the body does not like to be stressed, it deposits additional energy stores so that the next time you do this amount of work the body will have an ample reserve, which, in turn, allows you to do even more. This is known as supercompensation. But if you do not do sufficient work, your body will never get to the point of bringing about supercompensation, and you will merely recover or replace what was used up.

You probably experienced supercompensation when you first began to run. After your first run you were probably quite tired, but as you kept running, you eventually were able to run a particular distance without undue fatigue. Thus, in the very early stages of running, your body overcompensated. Not only did you gain extra energy but your muscles and support structures also grew and developed in relation to the workloads. This allowed you to do more and to do it more effectively. But once you were accustomed to running, your body merely replaced the energy supply that was used up and returned to its normal state.

If you want to improve your capabilities, you have to exert yourself physically to get a training effect. You need additional supercompensation for additional speed, strength, flexibility, endurance, and other physical qualities. Supercompensation is your ticket for making progress in your running and in your physical development.

For your running and exercise program to be most successful, you must have the fuels to make the needed body changes. To exercise and run without giving your body these required fuels adds one stress to another almost as blatantly as if you were trying to run your car without gas. Eating well is not difficult and does not require extensive record keeping. The key is not to count the calories but to choose a wide variety of the right kinds of foods, in the right amounts, and eat them at the right time of day.

Fat

Dietary fat has been on just about everyone's nutritional chopping block, with some legitimate reasons. Fat is calorically denser than protein or carbohydrates. A single gram contains nine calories, while a gram of protein or carbohydrate contains only about four. Diets high in saturated fat and trans fats appear to be a risk factor for obesity, heart disease, high blood pressure, stroke, diabetes, and even some forms of cancer.

A high-fat diet (especially of mostly saturated fat) typically leaves you feeling sluggish, so that you will not be able to play or exercise at your best. Also, consumed dietary fat has a pronounced tendency to become body fat. That is especially true of saturated fat, the kind found in fatty meats, full-fat dairy products, palm and coconut oil, and trans fats (hydrogenated oils) as found in margarine and many other

products. Studies show that diets high in saturated fat tend to produce body fat in the abdomen more than anywhere else.

Fat must never be eliminated or severely cut back from the diet, especially if you are a long-distance runner. The body needs fat for many functions, which include assimilating fat-soluble vitamins and manufacturing cell walls and certain essential enzymes and hormones. Fat also makes food more satisfying and filling. And, most important, it supplies the best energy for long-distance runs.

Try to limit your intake of dietary fat to about 25 to 30 percent of your daily caloric intake. Start simply by cutting down on the most obvious foods, such as fried foods, rich sauces, hamburgers, hot dogs, full-fat salad dressings, mayonnaise, and rich desserts. Use good oils, such as olive, canola, peanut, safflower, flaxseed, or walnut, and be very selective in your use of other fats.

An excellent way to get good fat is to eat raw nuts as a snack. And use butter instead of margarine. Even though the virtues of margarine have been extolled for many years, we now know that it results in many more negative effects than butter. Butter is a natural product the body can assimilate, while margarine, a trans-fatty acid, acts the same as a saturated fat and remains in your body for extended periods of time. Eat plenty of fish and fish oils, especially if you have a tendency to overdo saturated fat. Fish oils will move saturated fat out of the body.

Protein

Protein is very important as it provides the basic building blocks for cellular muscular repair and development, and it provides energy. While carbohydrates and fats supply most of the energy for muscular exertion, protein enables your muscles to respond to this exertion by getting firmer and stronger (and also supplies you—especially your brain—with energy!). This is why your need for protein increases the more you put your muscles to work. Exercise causes the muscles to undergo a type of intricate cellular breakdown that only protein can repair and build upon.

Running and being on a regular exercise program means you should be getting approximately one-half to one gram of protein daily for every pound you weigh (approximately 30 percent of your daily caloric intake). The exact amount will depend on your age, the intensity and duration of your workouts, and your level of development. Some of the best sources of protein are lean meats, poultry, fish, low-fat dairy products, whole-grain cereals and breads, beans, and nuts.

Carbohydrates

Carbohydrates are great for fast energy, and in some ways are the most healthful type of food you can eat. They include pastas, cereals, breads, potatoes, rice, beans, fruits, and vegetables. Carbohydrates should be eaten in their natural, "complex" forms. Potato chips and candy bars don't count!

The more energy you have, the more you'll maintain, which leads to high-quality runs and workouts. Some carbohydrates are unique: they rev up your body's metabolic rate, even when you're just resting, and once you begin to exercise, really kick into gear. But this benefit is of relatively short duration. If you run long distances, then fats (and some amino acids) are most important.

Note: According to clinical nutritionist, Dr. Tobin Watkinson, it appears that women do not react the same way to some carbohydrates as men. He has found that some women gain weight when they eat carbohydrates such as pastas, breads, and potatoes. Most men, however, do not react this way. This may explain why some people, especially women, often get sleepy after eating certain carbohydrates. Carbohydrates seem to react on some bodies the same way protein does on others. Because of this, it is important that you learn how your body reacts to different nutrients and eat accordingly.

Fiber

Fiber is the key to keeping your digestive system in shape. But fiber can also affect the shape of your body, mainly because fiber plays a role in excreting dietary fat. Get enough fiber in your diet and you help sweep dietary fat through your intestines before it has a chance to be fully absorbed. This spares not only your waistline, but also your arteries and heart. It is also important to note that the best sources of fiber are foods rich in high-energy carbohydrates (grains, potatoes, beans). Try to get approximately thirty grams of fiber a day, which is roughly twice the amount the average American routinely consumes.

Eating Hints

You don't have to look far to find the kinds of foods that will enable you to function at your best. For example, bread, cereal, rice, pasta, and vegetables are among the most nutritious foods. Grains are nutrient storehouses. Grains such as wheat, oats, brown rice, millet, rye, and barley are rich in vitamins and minerals, and provide great amounts of energy. No wonder grains, along with beans and legumes, serve as a staple for so many cultures.

To fulfill your quota of these valuable complex carbohydrates, think beyond the popular white rice and white-flour products. Choose from whole-grain products, and go for variety. Beware of baked goods. Cornbread, muffins, and pancakes made with whole grains and little fat are fine. But avoid fat-enhanced baked goods such as biscuits and high-fat quick breads. Read the labels on pastries, taco shells, and pancake mixes for fat content. And stay away from corn chips, donuts, potato chips, high-fat crackers, cookies, cakes, and sweet rolls.

Vegetables are another mainstay of your diet. When you make a salad, think beyond iceberg lettuce, which is practically devoid of any nutritional value. Use two or three different kinds of greens, such as spinach or romaine. Add items such as celery; green, yellow, or red peppers; red onions; broccoli; cauliflower; carrots; or any raw vegetable you enjoy. To further liven up salads, work in some foods from the grains and legumes group, and toss some peas or beans on your greens. Such salads can even be eaten without any dressing, which is usually loaded with bad fats.

In this way, you can consume hundreds of satisfying calories, while taking in minimal amounts of fat. Also keep a couple of sealed plastic bags of chopped raw veggies handy in your crisper. Broccoli, carrots, zucchini, cauliflower, asparagus, green or red peppers, pea pods, fresh green beans, chickpeas, mushrooms, turnips, and tomatoes are great for snacks.

Fresh fruit can quench your thirst and fill you up. Whole fruit is also a reliable source of fiber. Go for whole fruit, preferably locally grown and naturally ripened, since it is more satisfying and nutritious. Fruit in season is more likely to be fresh.

Milk, yogurt, and cheese are also important in your diet, along with meat, poultry, fish, beans, eggs, and nuts. As brought out before, protein is very important, but eat mostly lean meats to get your full complement of amino acids and less saturated fat. To fulfill your daily quota of this food group, concentrate on foods rich in high-quality protein, such as lean meats, poultry, beans, fish. Fresh raw nuts and seeds are an excellent source of protein, fiber, vitamins, and minerals.

Eggs are not the culprit in increasing cholesterol levels. The real culprit is the chicken feed! The feed is devoid of many products such as lecithin, the key to breaking up cholesterol and moving it through the body. In other words, the adulterated chicken food that is lacking in nutrients makes the eggs major sources of cholesterol! Natural eggs from free-range chickens will not give you higher cholesterol levels.

Fat-Free Foods

The number of fat-free foods has increased astronomically over the past few years, as have low-fat substitutes. However, studies show that people now eat more fat than they did before and are still gaining weight because they are eating more. Thus, the culprit is not simply eating food with fat. Best is to eat food with the fat in its natural state and not overeat.

Another drawback to eating low-fat and no-fat foods is that the reconstituted versions of the real

thing lack fat-soluble nutrients and possibly other undiscovered nutrients. Scientists are still discovering new vitamins and minerals that up until now were not thought to be important to human health! To be sure you are getting an adequate supply of everything you need, your diet should include foods that are as close as possible to their natural state, and that includes fat.

Don't rely on artificial sweeteners. Studies have found that over the course of a year, people who use artificial sweeteners are more likely to gain weight than non-users. The artificial sweeteners may increase feelings of hunger since the brain interprets all sweeteners equally and triggers changes in blood sugar that mimic a reaction to sugar.

Keep It Simple

When it comes to preparing food, less is better. Don't overcook vegetables or obliterate otherwise healthy foods with high-fat cooking techniques, such as deep-frying, or sautéing in gobs of lard or butter. It has been my experience that foods eaten as close as possible to their natural state provide maximum nutrition and taste with minimum fuss. So do yourself a favor: leave the time-consuming and calorie-adding gourmet cooking to French chefs. Try to appreciate foods for what they are as opposed to what they become once adulterated by some high-fat garnish or sauce, and you will be that much ahead of the game.

No Skipping Meals

If you are most active in the morning or early day, and like to retire early, your evening meal should be relatively light, while breakfast or lunch should be heavy. Eat at least three times a day. That's right, no skipping meals, and especially no fasting. Your body is a finely tuned machine that needs fuel on a regular basis.

The next time you are too busy to eat and don't have time for a conventional meal, there is nothing wrong with a healthful snack, such as a piece of fruit, a small sandwich, some nuts, or a container of yogurt. People who are successful in maintaining a normal weight find that, in addition to exercising regularly, they eat as many as five or six mini meals a day. The use of whole-food bars, such as the Standardbar™ by Standard Process, that contain a balance of various nutrients, vitamins, and minerals are also beneficial when there is insufficient time for a full meal to digest before a run, heavy practice, or competition. However, beware of food bars made from synthetic chemicals. They do not have the wholesome food benefits in whole-food bars.

Water

Water is extremely important to runners. It keeps you hydrated enough to exercise with maximum efficiency, and it helps your body cool itself and get rid of its natural waste products.

When you exercise, you lose water through sweat and breathing, and the losses can be substantial. This doesn't mean sweating is a negative; it is natural and desirable. Perspiration cools the body, gets rid of waste products, and cleanses the pores. But it also depletes the body of water that must be replaced. So play it safe and drink at least eight eight-ounce glasses of water a day, in addition to any soda, beer, coffee, or tea. (One rule of thumb suggests a liter a day for every fifty pounds you weigh.) And don't wait till you're thirsty to drink. Your body can be short of water without your thirst letting you know about it.

There are also some good waters on the market that can assist you in recovery after a workout. For example, Oxy-Water™ has added oxygen, five to seven times that of normal bottled waters. There are no other additives or chemicals, making it an ideal supplement when needed. Runners are finding it very effective for recovery between races and during long runs. When taken after a hard workout, the runners feel fully recovered the next day and also experience less soreness. It appears that the extra oxygen in the blood helps to quickly convert the lactic acid to adenosine triphosphate

(ATP), which is the basic form of energy used by cells. Oxy-Water™ also gets rid of more waste products.

Eat Food, Not Pills

I cannot overemphasize the importance of eating fresh and natural foods whenever possible. Don't let yourself be duped by the fantastic advertising claims often made for certain high-price foods or supplements, especially processed or synthetic. If you eat wisely and eat a variety of foods from the different categories you shouldn't need many additional supplements. Supplementation, as the term implies, is to supplement your diet.

If you find your diet lacking, your food sources are grown on land that is depleted of nutrients, or if there are environmental conditions that lower the value of foods, then supplementation becomes very important. As for health foods, there are none better than what you can make for yourself from natural, organic foods purchased as fresh as possible. Do not think of health foods as something only for extremists. Think of them as foods that keep you well and do not make you sick.

When you take supplements, be sure they are full natural complexes of the various vitamins and minerals. In nature, these vitamins and minerals are combined in varying degrees and should be eaten in their natural forms so the body can better assimilate them and get their many benefits. Beware of synthetic products, and especially synthetic vitamins, as they may actually create vitamin deficits and not give you what your body truly needs.

For example, the synthetic version of vitamin C consists of ascorbic acid. But ascorbic acid is only one component of the total vitamin-C complex, which contains other vitamins and minerals in order to be complete. Thus, when you take only ascorbic acid into the body, it will rob the body of other nutrients in order to become complete. If continued over a long period of time, it can deplete you of other vitamins and minerals.

One brand of whole-food vitamins, minerals, and other supplements that I have been using for many years and can strongly recommend is Standard Process. These products are sold through physicians and professionals to better guide in their use. Standard Process uses only organically grown products to make its supplements. Its products, which also include energy and meal-replacement bars, have made a substantial positive difference in many runners' performances and well-being.

Enjoy Your Food

With a little imagination and not a lot of work, you can make your healthy diet extremely enjoyable. If your diet isn't giving you pleasure, it is lacking in some aspect, regardless of how nutritionally complete it may be. It is also important to allow yourself some of your favorite foods because many food cravings are trying to tell you something about your body's chemistry. A craving for something sweet, for example, could be a sign that your blood sugar has fallen too low. (Don't make eating sweets a habit though.) Or a strong urge for something salty could mean the sweat you are losing in your workouts has caused your body's sodium levels to dip. Use natural sea salt to make up for any loss.

Learn to respect your body's messages if you are serious about running and working out, because they are usually telling you something you should know.

When you do partake in something a little special, don't feel guilty about it. Erase guilt from your vocabulary. If you are exercising regularly, the food will have a purpose. In fact, the more you run and exercise, the more you will automatically find yourself migrating to better and healthier foods, mainly because you will see the difference in your abilities and how you feel.

Special Nutritional Needs for Runners

For more running-specific nutritional information, I interviewed Dr. Tobin Watkinson, a renowned clinical nutritionist at the Scripps Clinic in Del Mar,

California. He noted that energy expenditure and nourishment for running depend largely on when you run and if you are a morning or night person. Because of this you must adjust your eating to meet the demands of the workout or competition.

Carbohydrates or Fats?

As you start your running or workouts, your energy levels are usually high. But as you move through your workout your body begins to burn different fuels. Initially you utilize a fair amount of the sugars (carbohydrates) that are present in your body from the stores of glycogen. Once you have depleted the sugar your body begins burning fat. Thus most runners probably burn sugar for the first few miles (runs or practice) and then more fat. As a result you may see a difference in your run or workout from beginning to end. Some runners actually feel the shift that occurs as the fuels change.

If you constantly take in carbohydrate-type drinks and other products to keep replenishing carbohydrate stores, your body will not be trained to utilize body fat. Fat is not automatically burned. Your body must adapt to burning fat. One way to do this is to run close to your anaerobic threshold. This is where you can get the greatest breakdown of fats, which supply much more energy than carbs per unit of use. However, if you limit the amount of fat you take in and constantly take in more carbohydrates and carbohydrate-type drinks during your run, your body will stop burning fat and will not be trained to utilize the fat in the body.

Fat is not automatically burned at the most efficient rate. You must train your body to adapt to burning fat to make your running most efficient. One way is to run fast enough to be at your anaerobic threshold and to sustain it as long as possible. Burning fat in this regime will give you much greater energy than carbohydrates, which will never be able to fuel you over a long distance at a relatively fast rate. Keep in mind that only through training to utilize more fat will you be able to go farther and faster.

The fact that your body relies greatly on fat to fuel your running is so obvious that it has been greatly overlooked. In the fitness literature, it is well recognized that if you wish to lose fat you must run longer distances and run faster. As you run faster and longer, your body utilizes the fat for energy, and as a result, you lose the fat stores and become thinner and lighter. Because of this I am always amazed at diets recommended for runners that contain mostly carbohydrates and very little fat.

As a result of these diets, it is not uncommon to find runners who look emaciated, are very thin, and have hardly any muscle (which is probably cannibalized for energy) and practically no fat stores. Runners who have an extremely high-carbohydrate diet with minimal fat train the body to run on carbohydrates as the main fuel rather than on fat, which is so much more efficient. This can also explain why some runners "hit the wall" in a long-distance run. They simply run out of carbohydrates and do not have sufficient fat stores for the body to use to supply energy. Or perhaps their bodies are unable to efficiently utilize fat as an energy source because of their overreliance on carbohydrates.

Without constant carbohydrate replenishment it is a proven fact that the body uses fat as its main fuel source in running long distances if the body has sufficient fat above its survival cache. Keep in mind that as you run out of carbohydrates, which get you started and supply the energy in the early phase of the run, and if you do not have an adequate supply of fat for the body to use, you will cannibalize muscle for additional energy supplies. This is why it is common to find many runners with minimal amounts of muscle, which can make them more prone to injury and lead to greater difficulty in completing the distance. Their muscles simply are not capable of doing the work needed.

These problems are even more compounded if your diet is extremely high in carbohydrates (60 percent or more). By taking in an insufficient amount of fat, especially good fat that can be utilized for energy, you end up taking relatively short runs, lasting only a few miles. The increased carbohydrates may be sufficient to fuel your runs, but they certainly do not train your body to utilize fat for the longer runs. This is the main reason I believe many runners who train for a marathon by running short distances and who have high carbohydrate stores cannot complete the marathon. They literally run out of gas.

Their bodies are unable to utilize fat, or they do not have a sufficient amount of fat for the body to use. You should also understand that the body will maintain a minimal amount of fat and cannibalize muscle before it will use up all the fat in the body.

Thus, I seriously question the practice of carbohydrate loading and maintaining an extremely high-carbohydrate diet. By doing this, you must rely on more and more sugar for energy instead of burning fat to provide twice the amount of energy. If you eat a more balanced diet and run to train your body to utilize fat, you may find your running efficiency improving tremendously.

You may have read about studies on high-fat diets and how they do not increase running performance. These studies are accurate, but they are also misleading. Merely taking in more fat does not mean your body will automatically adjust to burning more fat during the workout. You must train your body to do this. It needs time to adapt to burning different fuels and to make the necessary changes. A more balanced and varied diet is needed. To my knowledge there have been no U.S. studies to show the effectiveness of such diets. However, in my work with many athletes I have seen distinct improvement in running performance by eating a more varied and balanced diet with a more equal intake of carbohydrates and fats and proteins.

The Runner's Plan

The first step in creating a more efficient diet is to time your meals so that, if you are more of a morning person, you have your heavier starch, protein, and vegetables for breakfast. An omelet would be an excellent choice. The mid-morning snack should include nuts and seeds, proteins that keep your sugars up but don't give you an overabundance of carbohydrates. They will run your brain very well.

It is best to have nuts raw and unsalted, unless you are running in some very hot weather, at which time a little natural sea salt is good. In addition, eat only the nuts and seeds since they can be digested easily and more efficiently on an empty stomach. When nuts and seeds are cooked with salt and oil, they go bad easily and may cause headaches.

If you are an afternoon or evening person and run in the morning, you should start your day with fruit and then have a mid-morning snack of some more substantial protein such as beef jerky. Evening people need to have fruit in the morning to raise their blood sugar. If you have some fruit and then a vegetable snack later, you will do better.

For an afternoon run, lunch for a morning person or an afternoon person is basically the same. A morning person should have starch in the morning, and a night person should have starch at night. If you have too much protein at lunch, you'll get tired in the afternoon and soon find yourself yawning. Too much starch or protein will be converted to sugar, making them inappropriate choices for lunch. An appropriate lunch would be lots of above-ground vegetables, and a little protein such as fish or chicken. Do not have only pasta or a sandwich.

Drinking soft drinks or alcohol can be detrimental when working out. They will dehydrate you and affect your blood sugar. The sugary soft drinks and fruit juices that you might think would be great are, in fact, not very good. For example, how many real oranges does it take to make a glass of orange juice? Not many people would sit down and eat the four or five oranges that it takes to make a glass of orange juice. Eating the whole fruit is much better than just having the juice.

If you are a morning person you should have a snack of some fruit in the afternoon. If you are a night person, have nuts in the middle of the afternoon. You need the protein to make it through to dinner!

Keeping Hydrated

According to Dr. Watkinson, the only thing that can totally rehydrate cells is water. You can survive on colas, soft drinks, iced tea, or sparkling mineral waters, but they will not rehydrate cells the way water will. Water is the universal solvent. It enters the cell, rehydrates it, and carries the waste materials away. You will not get these results with other drinks because the pH in most drinks is inappropriate for the body. For example, carbonated drinks are very acidic, versus being alkaline, which the body prefers for rehydrating cells.

Many designer waters are touted as rehydration drinks. The unfortunate thing about these drinks is that they only contain one or two electrolytes and their major ingredient is some form of sugar. They may taste good at the moment but you will not feel very well twenty minutes to an hour later when you begin to lose your concentration.

It's best to have water containing minerals such as calcium, magnesium, potassium, and sodium as found in some natural spring waters. For example, Japan's micro-water rehydrates the body more easily than conventional water and is a powerful antioxidant, which eliminates the free radicals formed in running and working out. Other bottled waters today, such as Oxy-Water™, are proving effective in quenching thirst, rehydrating the body, and supplying some needed elements. In all cases, be sure that your water intake is sufficient to satisfy your body's needs, especially during and after a run.

Sadly, most tap water is basically a chemical bath—it is no longer "natural" water. Rehydration is very important to runners and you should drink plenty of water a day. Keep in mind that our bodies are about 80 percent water and need to have a continuous supply of good water.

Concentration

Runners or athletes who run a lot in their sport need to maintain their concentration throughout a race or game, especially near the end. Concentration is basically brain chemistry, a balance between your ability to utilize the fuel you have taken in and your ability to convert it into the appropriate brain chemistries. All the amino acids, which are the small building blocks of protein, are the precursors to building the brain chemistries we hear much about today. These include serotonin, melatonin, epinephrine, and norepinephrine, as well as other products our brains need to be able to function as needed.

If you are running or playing a sport and are under stress, you are going to use a higher amount of your brain fuels. If you are unable to replenish these fuels because you have burned up the raw material or do not have adequate raw material, your body will stall. If you have a high demand as, for example, when you are in a major event and your body is unable to get the appropriate fuels to do what is needed, you will be unable to concentrate.

Emotional needs require even more nutritional support. When there is a heavy emotional component (as when you are running in a major race, or playing in a championship game), you can burn up to 25 percent more calories than you did in practice.

This is why it is so important to be well fortified nutritionally.

Be sure to have a wide range of foods and to follow the guidelines that have been discussed. This means having vegetables, protein, nuts and seeds, and some fruit in order to get a full range of rich sources of all vitamins and minerals. Unfortunately, many people today are taking synthetic and incomplete vitamins that actually create vitamin deficiencies, which cause some of the mental fogs people get into at times. We are not as smart as nature in our ability to produce a complete nutrient.

CHAPTER
11

Designing Your Exercise Program

Strength Training

It is generally understood among sprinters that weight (strength) training can lead to greater speed and power. In long-distance running, however, the need for strength training has not been universally accepted. In fact, many runners and coaches still believe weight training will make them slower, decrease their flexibility, and lead to injury. These myths have persisted in running for many years and should be dispelled. Weight training, when done correctly, is a runner's ally.

Depending on the type of weight-training program you undertake, you can: (1) improve running technique, (2) increase stride length and frequency, (3) increase muscular and aerobic endurance, (4) prevent injury, and (5) increase speed.

By tailoring the weight-training program to fit your needs, you can develop any specific type of strength needed, including endurance strength, absolute and relative strength, speed strength, eccentric strength, explosive strength, and starting strength. This is why you should not think of strength training simply as a means of getting bigger or stronger. Think of it as a means of improving various aspects of your running.

How much time should you devote to strength development in an overall training program? The time factor is a major objection many runners and coaches have to a separate strength-development program. As a result, they often combine strength training with speed or endurance training through interval training—running up hills or stairs, and even running in snow or sand dunes. These programs are somewhat effective but they do not fulfill the goals of special strength training because they lack the key element, progressive overload.

Without progressive overload you cannot regulate the intensity of the loads so the muscle can respond with continual increases in strength. For example, merely running uphill, which is not even specific to running and can teach you bad habits, will not lead to greater levels of strength (except when starting). The more you run uphill, the more you develop muscular endurance (except when done with speed and explosiveness).

In my research, I've discovered that strength and endurance are related and are on a continuum. In the initial stages of training, both strength and endurance are developed simultaneously. However, they are both specific physical qualities, and to properly develop each requires a separate training program. There is no single exercise capable of simultaneously developing both these qualities (or others) to the level needed in running, especially sprinting.

As important as strength increases are, the main objective of running is to run faster and farther, not to become the strongest person in the race. You have only so much time and energy to train. Because of this, strength development based on your needs and the requirements of your race should be placed in its proper perspective in the overall training program.

Since specific strength is developed through specific adaptation to the demands you place on the muscle, overloading must be carried out in a progressive manner in order to constantly raise the level of strength. This is best done through the use of pulley weights, rubber tubing, or free weights (dumbbells and barbells). This equipment is most effective for developing strength in runners, and the total energy output is minimal when compared to climbing hills, heavy labor, or running itself. Weather conditions do not prohibit its use and resistance can be adjusted to your abilities.

Resistance training can be done at home with free weights and rubber tubing. The two most important advantages of using such equipment are:

1. The overload principle can be made progressive by the gradual increase of the resistance used, thereby assuring a continuity of strength gains in the desired actions or body areas.

2. Resistance training can develop strength in any or all of the muscles of the body according to the requirements of your running event. For example, strong hip flexors, which are highly specific to sprinters and long-distance runners, can only be developed to the optimal level by doing the thigh-drive exercise with progressive resistance increases.

For your exercise program to be most effective you must individualize it according to whether you are a recreational or competitive runner (player) and whether you are a sprinter, middle- or long-distance runner, or broken-speed runner as in soccer, lacrosse, basketball, and other team sports. Your strength-development program should be designed primarily to develop strength in those muscles that assist you in making the most effective use of your speed, skill, endurance, and tactics as required for maximum performance in your event. In addition, the amount of resistance you use, the kind and number of exercises you execute, and the number of sets and reps you use for each exercise depend on your mastery of the exercises and of running. However, keep in mind that as your level of fitness improves, you should move up to the next level of difficulty.

Getting Started

For beginners and those who have not worked out for months or years, it is necessary to first go through a learning and familiarization stage to accustom your body gradually to exercise without soreness or discomfort. To begin, read (and sometimes re-read) exactly how to do the resistance exercises. Have this book with you when you train. Since most of the key exercises can be done at home, you can do them at your leisure and with privacy.

Do one exercise for three to five repetitions with light resistance. When using rubber tubing, adjust the length so that you can execute the exercise easily through a full range of motion. This means that you do the exercise (up and down, or away and back) three to four times. Execute each repetition at a moderate rate of speed.

As you do the exercise, concentrate on exactly how you are doing it and how it feels. Recognize what each exercise feels like and which muscles are working. In this way you will gain a better feel for the movement and how it relates to running. After completing three to five repetitions, relax and then get ready for the next exercise. Read the description and then do several repetitions. Proceed in this manner until you do all the exercises selected.

You do not have to do every exercise described in this book for each aspect of running technique. When beginning, pick out exercises for your troublesome areas or the joint actions you would like to improve. Other exercises can be attempted the following week or as you get used to doing your core exercises. For example, a sample exercise program may include the following:

1. good morning
2. back raise
3. knee drive
4. heel raise
5. squat
6. leg pullback
7. reverse sit-up
8. biceps curl

If you desire greater improvement in particular actions, include even more exercises. However, for many runners this sample program is quite sufficient for the first two to four weeks, especially in regard to learning the exercises. It is important that you record each exercise and the number of repetitions done so you know exactly where you are on each exercise at the next workout.

Personalize Your Program

You are a unique individual and will respond to the exercises differently than someone else. This is why you should never copy what someone else is doing. Because someone you know may have responded quickly to certain exercises, it does not mean that your body will also respond in the same manner. This is especially true in the senior years.

If you copy someone else's program, regardless of how successful it is, you risk getting injured. Not only may the resistance be greater than what your muscles and joints can handle, but the way the exercise is executed by another person may not fit the way your body is designed to move. In these instances, there is a high likelihood of injury. Your program must be individualized, just as your running is very individual.

Schedule your resistance workouts so they are not done immediately before you run. An ideal situation would be to do the exercises in the morning and to run (or practice your sport) in the afternoon. If you prefer running in the morning, you should do the exercises in late afternoon or evening. The key here is to give yourself a few hours of rest and recovery in between. Do the exercises consistently and at a fairly regular time so that you have ample time for recovery and for your body to adapt to the exercises.

Reps and Sets

Keep adding one or two repetitions at each workout (or each week) until you reach fifteen to twenty repetitions. When you repeatedly reach twenty repetitions you will be ready to increase the resistance for that particular exercise. If you have not reached twenty reps in the other exercises, remain at the same level.

After a few weeks you will become more comfortable with the exercises and have greater confidence. Since you will be able to handle more resistance and execute more repetitions without any discomfort or trepidation, you may want to add other exercises at this time. If you experience soreness on any workout day or on the day after, it means you did too many repetitions or used too much resistance. When this happens, use the same or less resistance in the next workout to help your body recover. When you feel good, you can gradually increase resistance or repetitions.

At this time you should do only one set of each exercise. A set means doing a particular number of repetitions of one exercise one time. For example, if you do twenty reps of the squat, this constitutes one set of squats. If you then do an additional twenty reps or less, it is considered set number two.

Since the main purpose of the workout program at this time is to familiarize you with the exercises and to gradually have your body adapt to the exercises and the workout, only one set is needed. Doing more than one set will not produce greater results. A greater number of sets is needed as you progress and become more fit and have greater mastery of the exercises. This is where additional sets play their most important role.

Scheduling Workouts

You should work out three days per week, and your workouts should last a maximum of twenty to thirty minutes. That's right, twenty to thirty minutes! For a maximum of ninety minutes a week, you can gain sufficient strength and flexibility to enable you to run faster and longer. This is especially true of long-distance runners. Sprinters usually require more time because of the need for higher levels of speed-strength as well as strength.

You will reach fifteen to twenty reps fairly rapidly in some exercises, while in others progress may be much slower. This is perfectly normal since some muscles take longer to respond and certain exercises are easier to learn than others. For many individuals it takes one to two months to reach fifteen to twenty reps in all the exercises.

It is important that you work out on a regular basis. You must not skip days and say, "I will do four days next week because I only did two this week." This is not effective. Working out more than three days per week does not bring additional benefits, and can lead to overtraining and the possibility of injury and soreness. A three-day program allows for a day's rest in between to give your muscles ample time to fully recover. As a result, it will not interfere with your running! When you are more fit, working out four to six times per week can be successfully integrated with your running.

To get maximum benefit from the strength-training program, you should continue running to constantly make minor adjustments in how you run. Most changes will be made unconsciously because of the muscular feel developed when doing the exercises. The changes will feel very natural to you! You should not be doing all-out sprints at this time. This may lead to injury as well as disrupting concentration on your form or technique changes.

Increasing Difficulty

When you reach fifteen to twenty reps for each exercise, and the exercises become "easy," you will be ready to make changes. At this time your workouts will become more strenuous. If you are already strong and have been working out, you should begin on this level, especially if you are familiar with the exercises. However, when starting a new exercise, begin as previously described and gradually build up to the level needed.

Regardless of whether you use rubber tubing, dumbbells, or barbells, when you reach about twenty reps, regularly increase resistance. Doing this

should bring you down to twelve to fifteen reps. Then work back up to twenty reps and repeat the process. When you do an exercise for fifteen to twenty reps it is important that the last repetition be the most you can do with proper technique. Do not, for example, do fifteen or twenty repetitions and still feel refreshed. When you finish the set you should feel slightly out of breath and have muscular fatigue.

Be in tune with your body as you do the exercises. Only in this way can you find out what is working for you and determine which exercises appear most effective. You can then make the necessary changes in the exercises or exercise program to produce the desired results. If you need more work on certain muscles, add another set to selected exercises.

Making Workouts More Specific

You can change your running significantly, depending on which exercises you use, and how many repetitions and sets. Thus how you set up your program at this time is critical to your success. Most important is that you make your workout specific to your event and the changes you desire.

Keep in mind that your workout program for strength is different from what it will be for producing increases in speed strength, and significantly different from a program aimed at increasing speed or endurance. In essence, workouts must be geared toward the qualities you desire to improve and the role they play in your particular event.

Long-distance runners may find great success from doing only one or two sets of fifteen to twenty reps to significantly improve their performance. Greater strength at this time will not be as important as raising the levels of muscular and cardiovascular endurance, which play much more important roles. A sprinter, on the other hand, needs greater levels of strength (both eccentric and concentric) as well as greater levels of speed strength, starting strength, and explosive strength. Thus the programs for both types of runners must be distinctly different, yet include some of the same exercises.

Developing Greater Strength

To increase strength you should do two to four sets of the key exercises. Using greater resistance at this time (which is needed for greater strength) requires a warm-up or initial preparation of the muscles. For the first set (when doing three or more sets), do ten repetitions with half the resistance you will be using in set two. In set two, do eight to ten reps for strength. Follow this with set three in which you do fifteen to twenty reps for muscular endurance.

After you do the first set, rest for thirty to sixty seconds for recovery. Then repeat the same exercise for the second set. You can also do another exercise for different muscles in between sets so that you can do more exercises in a shorter amount of time. If you have a very intense program, as is often needed with sprinters, a split program may be beneficial. This means you do the upper- and lower-body exercises twice a week on alternate days, with a day of rest for each. For example, Monday and Thursday—upper body; Tuesday and Friday—lower body; Wednesday and Saturday—special workouts for other qualities such as flexibility, agility, coordination, etc.

Completing three to four sets—a set for warm-up, one to two sets for strength, and a set for endurance—is usually sufficient for most runners. Most important is that you do the key exercises that will improve your weak actions and enhance your strong points. All your exercises should be very specific to your running (after you have developed a well-conditioned base).

There is no need for very great resistance in this program, unless you are a sprinter. Keep in mind that if you use too much resistance, your range of motion will decrease, which in turn can negatively affect your run. Be sure you do the exercises exactly as described regardless of how many sets or repetitions.

Speed-Strength and Explosive Training

Strength coupled with speed is most important for sprinters and open-field runners (as in football, soccer, lacrosse, and basketball). This type of training is needed to increase speed and quickness.

Speed-strength and explosive training should be done only after you have a well-established strength base. Some forms of explosive training, such as introductory plyometrics, can be done without a high level strength base because the explosive work is not intense and consists mainly of jump exercises, which are usually quite safe. If you do strength training three times a week, speed-strength work is done on the alternate days but no more than twice a week (three times a week if the workouts are relatively easy).

The introduction of explosive and speed-strength work for sprinters and open-field runners should be slow and gradual. It should begin with easy preparatory jump exercises as well as combinations of strength and explosive movements, such as holding a squat position for four to five seconds and then exploding upward. To ensure that you introduce the explosive work slowly and gradually, you should begin with activities such as simple skipping, hopping, jumping, leaping, and bounding. These activities prepare the muscles for more intense work later.

If you are on a four-day split program, then speed-strength work can be sequenced with strength training. In this case, speed-strength work is done first (after a vigorous warm-up) and the workout ends with strength and perhaps endurance work. Depending on your level of fitness and mastery of the exercises, the gradual buildup should last anywhere from three to eight or more weeks.

When you are capable of correctly doing a full-fledged depth jump, you will be ready for a maximum-intensity workout. At this time you should gradually increase the number of exercises that are done explosively. Begin with only a few exercises and then build up the number of exercises or the number of sets done for each exercise. Be sure you do each exercise correctly to get maximum benefits and prevent injury.

Long-distance runners should use speed-strength and explosive training sparingly. Keep in mind that aerobic capabilities are most important for long-distance runners. Up to 90 percent of training should be devoted to improving aerobic capabilities and muscular endurance. Speed work should comprise about 10 percent of the workouts. Strength training and some easy plyometrics play a major role here but only for a relatively short period of time and usually a month or so before major competitions. Long-distance runners should do only three to four speed-strength or lead-up plyometric exercises for one to two sets in the training session. These exercises should precede the strength or endurance training.

For sprinters, the intensity of the work is very high when doing speed-strength and explosive training. Because of this, more rest is needed between repetitions, making the workouts at this time longer than usual. They can last up to two or more hours, especially when followed by strength training. This type of training should be done only in the specialized period of training. Because this type of training has a strong residual effect, you should stop such training at least one to two weeks before major competitions to give the muscles ample time to adapt and be ready for all-out performance.

Speed Training

Speed training, which consists mainly of all-out sprinting, should be done no more than two times a week. Other aspects of speed work, such as starts, acceleration, stride running, etc., can be done more than twice a week. When speed training, you should have ample rest between sprints—up to seven or eight minutes, especially when doing 100-meter repeats.

In sprinting it is important to maintain the same running technique. When fatigue sets in, your technique changes and you begin to develop different neuromuscular pathways. However, when the nervous system is fresh you can duplicate exactly the correct technique to ensure the fastest running. Because of this, speed work should always precede other types of training. And the same holds true for explosive work. You should have ample rest between exercises or sets so the muscles are always capable of maximum contraction when doing the most intense forms of explosive training. Explosive exercises should never be done when you are fatigued.

If you are in the process of changing or modifying your technique, it is important that you not do all-out speed training. Once you master the necessary technique you can gradually begin to increase speed while still maintaining good running technique. If you do all-out running or speed running when trying to modify technique, you will inadvertently go back to your old sprint form, which will greatly interfere with any changes you are trying to make.

Do not do all-out speed training when you are also doing very heavy weight training. The two are not compatible. Very intense strength training should be decreased and speed-strength training increased as you begin to introduce all-out speed training. Doing speed work is best when you have already completed the strength-training phase and are moving into the speed and explosive phase. In this situation you can do some explosive exercises to better prepare the muscles for all-out sprinting.

Overspeed training can also be done at this time. When doing overspeed training you actually run faster than you can volitionally. Such training is very important for teaching the nervous system what it is like to go faster, which is needed to help you break your personal record. There are various ways of achieving overload, but the application of each method must be quite precise. For example, in downhill running, distance must not be too great and the slope angle must be within certain limits. Running with a parachute or extra weight is also effective, but how much weight and where it is distributed on the body play extremely important roles. Also important is the distance being run.

There is some new, relatively simple equipment being developed that can improve speed. One such product is the Springbakä Springsoles. These soles go in the shoe and, when you stand on them, you become stronger. When running, they allow for up to a 70 percent return of energy. This in turn improves your running speed significantly. For more information, call 877-777-4648.

Each of these methods requires considerable detail and great precision, and it is easy to overdo such training or misinterpret how the training should be done. For these reasons, and in an aim to prevent injury, they are not discussed in detail in this book. If you feel you are ready for such training (especially if you are involved in sprints), contact Sports Training for additional information. (See Appendix.)

Integrated Training

Athletes in most sports must work on more than simply improving one quality, such as speed. At times they must do separate training for strength, flexibility, neuromuscular coordination (technique), speed strength (power), muscular strength, cardiovascular endurance, and so on. How to integrate these different workouts into one or more training sessions becomes very important, especially in view of the limited time you may have. In general, the following is the order in which different physical qualities should be worked on in one session.

1. *Technique or Skill Learning.* In order to most effectively learn new technique or to modify technique, your nervous system must be in a high-energy state. In essence you must be alert and aware of exactly what you are doing. You must be tuned in to the feedback you receive and capable of making the changes needed to improve the actions desired. Because of this, technique must be first in your training.

2. *Speed and Explosive Training.* If no technique work is done, speed and explosiveness move to the top position. However, before undertaking such work it is important that you have an adequate warm-up to prepare the muscles for the high intensity encountered. If you wish to do both technique and speed work in the same session, the amount of technique work should be minimal. It should be used mainly to reinforce particular coordinations and as a warm-up to the speed and explosive training.

3. *Specialized Strength Work.* All exercises for strength that duplicate particular aspects of your skill technique must be done prior to other types of strength training. At this time you must be relatively fresh and energetic so you can concentrate on developing the muscular feel of the movement. Thus specialized strength work follows speed and explosive work, but only if you are not fatigued.

4. *General All-Around Strength Training.* Training that is not specific to the actions involved in running (general conditioning) can be done when you are fatigued. It should follow other types of training

that require maximum levels of energy. This type of training is often done after practice.

5. *Muscular and Cardiovascular Endurance.* Usually these two qualities are combined, but they can also be separate. For example, there are instances when you must work on muscular endurance as needed in a long-distance race. Such workouts are localized to particular joint actions. Cardiovascular work may automatically be included if it involves large body parts.

In cardiovascular work the total body is usually involved (cross-country running, cycling, and rowing). Endurance should always be the last type of training done in the session. It should never be used as a warm-up. Light jogging in which the heart rate stays well below the training zone is acceptable for warm-up, but to have a training effect in endurance work you must maintain your heart rate in the range where it will produce results. For example, for relatively young eighteen- to thirty-year-old athletes to produce an aerobic training effect the heart rate should be in the range of 140 to 160 beats per minute. For a combination training effect of aerobic and anaerobic capabilities the heart rate should be 160 to 180 beats per minute. To develop the anaerobic system the heart rate should be in the upper range of 180 to 200 beats per minute.

Maintaining Speed, Strength, and Endurance

It is not necessary to continually increase your strength or muscular endurance levels. This is especially true if you are a recreational runner. Maintaining your developed strength or endurance level is most important. Keep in mind that if you cease your workouts and only run, you'll lose some of the gained strength and endurance. This in turn will affect your speed, the distance you are capable of running, and your running technique. And it may lead to injury.

It is also necessary to keep in mind that continual increases in strength or other physical qualities are typically not called for during the season. This is especially true for athletes involved in sports such as football, baseball, soccer, lacrosse, etc. In season, maintaining the same technique for accuracy and developing a strategy based on one's physical and technical abilities become most important for winning success. All technique changes and increases in physical qualities should take place prior to the season.

Runners, especially sprinters, continue to do speed work in season to improve running speed. They also engage in overspeed, resistive and lightened running, towing, and other forms of work to bring about even greater gains in speed. However, because of the amount of speed work done, the amount of strength training is decreased or stopped to prevent injury. Usually speed and explosive training will maintain the achieved strength levels.

Long-distance runners, on the other hand, may continue to do muscular-endurance work, especially if it duplicates exactly what they do in their running stride. However, if they are seriously competing in different events, then the amount of strength or endurance training is minimal and ceases a week or so prior to any major competition.

For most runners who run recreationally, once a level of strength and endurance is developed that enables them to run at a sufficiently fast rate to achieve their fitness and health goals, additional increases in strength and muscular endurance are not needed. Maintaining speed strength and endurance is all that is called for. If you want to become faster or run farther, you should increase your levels of strength or endurance. But if you are happy with your present state you should merely maintain it.

To maintain your level of strength or endurance, continue to work out one to two days a week. Do one set of each exercise to maintain your running abilities. In some cases two sets may be needed. The number of repetitions will vary depending on your fitness level and goals. For most long-distance runners, doing one set of the key strength and endurance exercises for ten to twenty reps is usually sufficient when done twice a week. Sprinters usually require more work to maintain speed, especially if they are not doing speed and explosive work, which should maintain achieved strength levels if it is sufficiently intense.

If you stop training and only run (or if you do not exercise to maintain your fitness levels), you may find your running technique changing. This is especially true as you age. But by maintaining your strength and flexibility levels, you will be able to maintain the ability to run basically the same way in later years as in your youth. Increase your physical abilities and you will run on a higher skill level.

Training Principles

Working out can mean many things to different people, but how you work out is critical to your development. To get the maximum results, you should adhere to the following principles of exercise:

1. Individualization.   You are a unique individual. Aside from obvious structural differences there are also physiological differences in the muscular, circulatory, and nervous systems that require differences in your program. This is why you must be the one to make the final decision as to exactly which and how many exercises are needed, and how many sets and reps should be done. Your training program should be for you and only you.

Even though you cannot change your genetic makeup (which only determines one-third of your potential), you can greatly modify your speed, strength, flexibility, and other qualities. I have worked with many athletes who have literally transformed their bodies and their running abilities. Some started off fairly lackadaisical but ended up being the most active exercisers (and runners) I have ever seen.

2. Gradualness.   Regardless of your exercise program or level of performance, any increases in speed, flexibility, strength, resistance, repetitions, or sets should be very gradual. For example, if you are accustomed to doing fifteen reps for two sets, you should not in one day change to fifty or sixty repetitions or do four sets. Your body is not ready for such abrupt changes and injuries may occur. To prevent injury and maximize your results, all gains should be gradual.

3. *Progressiveness.* In order to continually show increases in speed, muscular strength, and endurance, you must progressively but gradually increase the amount of resistance, the number of exercises, or the total number of repetitions used. If you continue working at the same level and do the same number of exercises, sets, and reps, you will only maintain your achieved fitness level.

4. *Overload.* Overload means you do more than your body is accustomed to. In order to develop greater strength you must use additional resistance. To increase flexibility you must increase your range of motion. Other ways to achieve overload include increasing the rate of work, i.e., doing the exercises at a slightly faster rate of speed or in an explosive manner. These methods, however, apply more to sprinters and should be used only after you have achieved base levels of strength and endurance. They include plyometrics, explosive, and other speed-strength exercises.

5. *Awareness.* The principle of awareness is very important. To be aware, you should keep a record of your workouts. Record the resistance, sets, and repetitions for each exercise, and how you feel. Make notations of what you experience, both mentally and physically.

This is especially important for women who respond differently in each phase of the menstrual cycle. Some women do their best work (or running) before or after menstruation, while others perform better at the actual time of menstruation. Women should determine when they can do their most productive work and schedule the workouts (and running) around the menstrual cycle. In general, stay away from very strenuous activity (such as using heavy resistance) during the menstrual period.

Awareness also means being cognizant of what is happening to your body. You should learn what each exercise feels like and how your body responds to it. In time you develop muscle memory so that when you execute the exercise (or running technique) you can tell immediately if it is working for you or if something is amiss. When things do not feel right, you should check to see if your execution is correct or if there is some other problem.

6. *Consistency.* Without consistency in your exercise program, all the work you do may come to naught. For example, after each workout your energy supply is used up. It is replaced while you are resting and sleeping, and when additional energy supplies for later use are deposited. This is known as supercompensation. If you do not exercise sufficiently to use the extra energy that has been deposited, the body will re-absorb it and you may be left with the same energy as before. I am sure you have noticed that when you have not run for a while or have become sedentary you actually become more tired than if you were active throughout the entire day.

Consistency, which means doing the exercises on a regular basis, is the key to success in any exercise or running program. What I recommend, therefore, is that you block off the time needed in your busy schedule so that the exercise program becomes as important as all your other activities. If for some reason you are unable to work out for a week or two, start your exercises again upon your return, using less resistance. In one or two days you should get back into the groove of doing the exercises and seeing the results. Do not be overly concerned when situations arise that interfere with your program, but do not allow this to happen on a regular basis.

If you want to improve your running most effectively and in the shortest amount of time, schedule the exercises you should do. Once you set up a regular exercise program you will see the benefits quite soon. And you will become hooked. You will look forward to doing the exercises because you will see what the exercises are doing for you and how they are improving your running. You will also experience greater confidence in yourself, which will show up in better running and in everyday life.

Periodization

You now have the information needed to construct your individualized training program. To assist you in how the workout should be distributed throughout the year, it is important to understand the concepts of periodization and cycling.

In periodization, the year is divided into different periods or training phases. In each phase you train in a specific manner to gain certain physical qualities or attain certain results. The development you achieve enables you to do the training called for in the next period. The positive changes you experience from each training period make it possible for you to tackle the next phase, which eventually leads to your ultimate goal.

Because the goals of different athletes vary, so must the training periods and the types of training done in each period. Runners usually have trifold objectives: increase muscular strength and endurance, increase speed-strength capabilities to get more speed, and increase cardiovascular fitness for more endurance. Thus training is divided among technique, strength, endurance, and speed. These objectives are accomplished while maintaining—and in some cases increasing—flexibility. Training must be integrated in a manner that will ensure results in the allocated amount of time.

The Periodization Plan

In running there are usually two major competitive seasons, depending on whether you are a competitive or recreational-competitive runner. Most scholastic runners have two seasons, indoor and outdoor, or winter and summer (spring) seasons. As a result there should be two major competitive periodization plans, which should be basically the same. Keep in mind that all periodization plans follow the same pattern regardless of how long each plan lasts. Also, since the objectives in each competitive cycle are basically the same, the periodization plan will also have the same objectives and basic training methods employed.

In many schools a different periodization plan is employed, which is fairly common but which I believe is now outdated. In this periodization plan, all runners do cross-country running in the fall and speed or long-distance running in the spring or summer season. Cross-country running is good preparation for distance runners but it is not good preparation for sprinters and intermediate-distance runners.

All runners must develop a strong aerobic base before training for anaerobic improvement. Thus doing cross-country or long-distance running in the early stages of childhood running is advantageous, especially when looked at as part of a multi-year training program. However, as the youngster approaches twelve to fourteen years of age, then cross-country running is not as important for sprinters. Some long-distance running is advisable but it should be for shorter periods of time, depending on the level of aerobic fitness.

If runners are going to specialize in sprints, they must train on a year-round basis, with two periodization plans to prepare for sprints. Doing long distances at this time trains the explosive fibers to react slowly, which is good for endurance but not effective for sprinting. To be a sprinter you must train for sprinting. It is highly specific.

How Periods Are Broken Down

The periodization plan has four periods that can last three or more months. The four phases are general conditioning, specialized training, competition, and the post-competitive period.

For long-distance runners it is often difficult to pinpoint one major competitive season since there are long-distance races throughout the year. Because some runners try to run in as many races as possible it is extremely difficult to set up a true periodization plan. Suffice to say that running many races during the year is not a very effective way to train or improve performance.

The more you run and avoid other types of training, the greater your chances for injury. Running does not improve your physical abilities. You must train separately to improve strength, speed, and explosiveness, and then incorporate them into your running. Just running is a very poor way to improve performance.

If you are a long-distance runner, I strongly urge you to pick out the major races in which you wish to do your best. Other races, if you do participate in them, should then become training races and you should not be concerned with your times (except if it is a pre-set objective) or where you place. Do not select more than four major races per year, especially if they are spaced equally apart. If there are two or three races within a three- or four-month period, you can consider this your competitive period and break the rest of the year up into training phases.

Exactly how you break down your periodization plan depends on how often you compete and where and when you wish to do your best. Remember this is why you undergo a periodization plan—to do your best at a particular time in a specific race. It is the only way you can achieve better performances than you have had in the past.

Phase 1—General Physical Preparation. The initial stage of training consists of general preparatory or conditioning exercises to strengthen all the major muscles and joints to prepare you for the more intense training to follow. This period is also used to rehabilitate injured muscles and joints, and to strengthen or bring lagging muscles up to par. The work in this period is very general in nature to avoid building up psychological stress. You accustom your body to working out with different exercises and activities, and the volume of work done is very high but the intensity is low. In essence you use this period to prepare your body for future training. Aerobic and general strength training are most important here. For some runners, technique work is also important at this time.

The exact length of time spent in this phase depends on your mastery of the exercises and running technique, your fitness level, sex, age, and so on. The younger or more novice you are, the more time you should spend in this phase of training in order to increase strength and other physical qualities. For beginners this phase can last three to four months.

If you are a high-level runner you may spend two to four weeks in this period, mainly to prepare your body to do more intense training. This is based on the assumption that you remain in good physical condition and that you have maintained your running skills throughout the year. On this level you do not lose your running form from the previous year.

For most runners, this period lasts approximately four to eight weeks.

The general all-around strength program should include many varied strength exercises. For most runners, some of the best lower-body exercises are the heel raise, toe raise, squat, hip abduction and flexion, the good morning, and the glute-ham-gastroc raise. These exercises develop the leg and hip muscles in their different actions, which are most important for running and injury prevention.

Midsection exercises include the 45-degree sit-up (crunch), reverse sit-up, reverse trunk twist, and back raise. These exercises play a very important role in strengthening the back to prevent injury and in developing the abdominal muscular corset needed for a powerful midsection, which is especially important for sprinters.

Upper-body exercises include the bench press, pullover, full-range lateral and front arm raise, reverse fly, biceps curl, triceps extension, and shoulder extension. These exercises improve arm action and help attain strong, flexible, and relaxed shoulders.

Not all runners have to do every single exercise. You should first determine your strong and weak points and then do the exercises needed to improve your weak points, making you more balanced in your overall development. However, do not neglect your strong points. They must still be improved, but the amount of work done on your strong points at this time should be less than what you do for the lagging aspects of your muscle strength.

Phase 2—Specialized Physical Training. The specialized physical training period begins gradually as the general preparatory period comes to an end. In this way there is a smooth transition from general to specific training.

In specialized physical training, the work becomes very specific to running. This means practicing specific joint actions and using exercises for increasing strength and speed-strength exactly as needed in running. The exercises also duplicate the same range of motion and type of muscular contraction used in running. Thus the exercises enhance your running greatly and you can see results very quickly.

Your exact workout at this time depends on your level of ability and stage of training. If you are a novice or out of shape, then a sample program can consist of some of the following exercises, which are explained in detail in Chapters 6 and 7:

- heel raise
- explosive heel raise
- squat
- good morning
- glute-ham-gastroc raise
- back raise (to also prevent back injury)
- leg pullback
- knee drive
- jump out of a squat
- other plyometric (explosive) exercises

More advanced or high-level runners (especially sprinters) may have a similar program. But they usually include more sets of explosive exercises or use a split program to do lower-body, upper-body, and total-body explosive exercises together with specialized strength exercises to enhance particular actions. A sample program may be as follows:

Monday and Thursday:
- power skips
- jumps out of squats
- double-leg explosive jumps
- single-leg explosive jumps
- ankle jumps

These exercises are done for one to three sets of five to ten repetitions. They are then followed by lower-body strength exercises.

Tuesday and Friday:
- bent-arm raises
- explosive triceps extensions
- fast straight- and bent-arm pulldowns

These exercises are done for two to three sets of five to ten repetitions. They are followed by upper-body strength exercises.

On Wednesday and Saturday specialty work is done for specific skills, such as starts, or developing a big kick at the end of a race. The exact work depends on your objectives and your specific needs. For example, these days can also be used for greater abdominal and lower-back strengthening, concentrating on the rotational muscles. Exercises should include Yessis Back Machine sit-ups (two variants), reverse trunk twists, back raises with a twist, etc.

Since most of you should be working on greater increases in strength and speed it is very important that you integrate training so you can include all the different types of training in a timely and effective manner. You do this specialized work as you get closer to competitive running. By the end of this period of training you should be ready to begin competition.

Phase 3—The Competitive Period. In the ideal situation, during the competitive period your training should be devoted to maintaining the physical qualities you've already developed and perfecting your technique. You should not be increasing strength at this time because doing so will affect your technique.

The main focus in the competitive period should be on perfecting running technique, increasing speed, and developing the psychological and strategic aspects of the race. These three aspects should be worked on together during the competitive period, with actual execution of the competitive run in the sprints but only portions of the total run in long-distance running. However, keep in mind that your physical abilities should have been developed to their optimal levels during the specialized training period.

Because the actual training workouts at this time depend to a great extent on your coach, no details are presented here. Suffice it to say that your race strategies should be developed in practice.

Phase 4—The Post-Competitive Period. After competition you should go through a stage of recuperation and relaxation, especially from a mental standpoint. At this time your body can still do physical work but your mind must rest. Active rest is best. This means you remain active for relaxation purposes, not for physical development. At this time it is beneficial to participate in a different active sport that you enjoy so you can experience physical work but also get pleasure and satisfaction from a different activity. The post-competitive period usually lasts two to four weeks, depending on the length of your running season and how long it takes you to wind down.

If you are relatively weak and need greater strength you can immediately go into a strength-training program to improve your capabilities. The more time you spend developing strength, the more you will be able to convert to speed and explosiveness (or endurance) to get ready to compete and be on a par with higher-level runners.

By using the schematic presented here it is possible to achieve the highest levels of physical and sports performance in running. Each training period builds on the previous period and allows for the best performance during the competitive period. Equally important to ensuring that you get the most out of each training period is the periodization of your nutrition. It is critical to eat and supplement according to the training you are doing. See Chapter 10 for additional details on nutrition.

Avoid Early Burnout

If you reach your top performance in the shortest amount of time (one to two months), you'll find it almost impossible to maintain top sports form for any appreciable length of time. This happens to many runners who reach their peak early. When major competition comes they are already burned out or begin to stagnate so they can no longer perform at their best. This situation can easily be avoided.

You must take each period of training in progression and let your body develop in a natural manner. Then when you peak you will be at your best, capable of performing better than you have ever performed before. Do not just run, and do not overtrain, and you will be able to start the next training cycle fresh and healthy. This way you can again experience great gains for an even better season the following year.

This periodization system is extremely effective. I have been amazed by runners who have shown tremendous improvement in running speed without doing any speed training. They mainly work on special strength and explosiveness to prepare their muscles to act the way they must in sprinting or long-distance running. When they begin sprinting (or long-distance running), they run faster than ever before. The amount of improvement, especially with runners at the beginning of such training, is truly outstanding. The gains become even greater when speed work is incorporated into the program.

Cycling

Cycling means repeating the same skill or exercise over and over, for example, the leg action in running. In essence you repeat a certain number of repetitions for a certain period of time.

Cycling also means repeating the same workout to produce a training effect—to achieve physiological changes in the body from the training you do. If you continually keep changing your training program every week or every day, your body will not have a sufficient amount of time to attain the training effect. The body adapts or increases in strength and other physical qualities only when there is repetition of a particular stimulus for a certain amount of time. The stimulus in this case is the workout or the exercises you are doing. You can add additional resistance, but the exercises and number of sets and reps should remain the same.

After your body adapts to the workout program a change is needed. You cannot keep repeating the same exercises or exercise routines over and over because the body will rebel in time. The same routine "deadens" the nervous system so the muscle gains cease, and in some cases, decrease.

When a particular exercise or routine is repeated over too long a period of time, there is stagnation (depletion of nervous-system energy) and the muscles are no longer stimulated to respond. This is a catch-22 situation. You must keep doing the exercises or routine the same way for a certain period of time to get the maximum benefit, but going beyond this time brings about negative changes.

So you must, at the right time, change the routine to get renewed energy and continued growth. The key to success is in knowing when to make the necessary changes in order to restimulate the central nervous system. This is possible only if you keep detailed diaries of your workouts. See sample record sheet on page 158. A record-keeping book is also available.

Sample Record Sheet

Date: Time: Objective: Training Period:

| Exercise | Set 1 | | Set 2 | | Set 3 | | Set 4 | |
	Reps	Resistance Cord color or weight	Reps	Resistance Cord color or weight	Reps	Resistance Cord color or weight	Reps	Resistance Cord color or weight
1								
2								
3								
4								
5								
6								
7								
8								
9								
10								
11								
12								
13								
14								
15								
16								
17								
18								
19								
20								

Self-Assessment

Other Information:

In general, high-level and fit runners must change some basic exercises, such as the squat and bench press, every four to six weeks in order to see constant gains. Beginners and intermediates, however, may continue to experience gains for up to three to four months! There is a wide gap between different levels of runners. When specific exercises are considered, you can see even greater variability. Because of this you need a differentiated approach and it must be geared to your level of fitness and exercise and running mastery.

When cycling your workouts you should not have five days of very intense workouts in a row. Most often you should have a hard day followed by an easy or a moderate day, alternating in this manner over the week. When getting ready to peak, or getting ready for competition, it is possible to have two or three heavy days in a row followed by some light days. Also, after every three weeks or so—especially if the workouts are fairly intense—you should have a relatively light to moderate workout week to allow your body more time for full adaptation to take place, to help the body recover, and to prevent overtraining.

Many runners want a daily prescription detailing what they should do for every workout. But this is impossible because each workout, and the exact amount of time you do each exercise or program before changing the workout routine, must be based on individual abilities.

12

Tips to Maintain
Your Running Program

Many runners are successful in initiating an exercise program but tend to keep it up for only relatively short periods of time. Because of this, they rarely see all the positive results that are possible. To prevent this from happening to you and to help you maintain your program, here are some time-proven tips that have worked successfully for many runners:

1. Schedule Exercise First. Exercise and running should come first. This may seem heretical as it appears to take away from your job, schoolwork, and other extremely important chores. However, setting a time aside when you will exercise is a key element for success. Maintaining your exercise program will improve your mental work, making you more efficient and productive, which then allows you to get more done. This saves time, makes you feel better, and allows you to run better. Putting in exercise and sports participation only when you have time will doom you to defeat.

2. Adopt an Exercise Lifestyle. Exercise and running should be a part of your healthy lifestyle. In essence, you must develop the habit of participating on a regular basis. Once the habit is established it is very difficult to break. But in order to establish the habit, it must become a part of your normal, everyday routine.

3. Give Your Workout a Fair Chance. First exposure to any exercise or training program can be uncomfortable. This also holds true for many other areas of life. But continuing the activity and getting effective instruction in the basic techniques eventually can lead to enjoyment and pleasure. Few activities are truly enjoyed from the first day of participation; you must learn to enjoy them!

4. Start Slowly. Your body needs time to adapt in order for the gains to be seen and, most important, for the gains to last. Progress in the program can be fast but any increases in volume, intensity, exercises, etc., should be slow and gradual.

5. Keep It Individualized. Your training program must be individualized to fit you. This means you should make progress at your own rate and that the training program must be based on your capabilities—not someone else's.

6. Just Do It. People are great at making up excuses for why they cannot work out. They procrastinate and say they will do it at a later time. This is acceptable at times, but chronic procrastination can defeat all your good intentions. One or two missed workouts can be quickly made up. But if you start skipping more days, it is important to figure out why and what steps can be taken immediately. Procrastinating jeopardizes the success of any program, and it is stressful and lowers your self-esteem, further snuffing your motivation to stick with the program.

7. Keep a Workout Diary.   When you keep a diary of your workouts, either by yourself or in conjunction with others, it can be used to evaluate your progress. The diary should show if progress is commensurate with your abilities and if any problems are developing along the way. See sample record sheet on page 158.

8. Forget About Being Perfect.   Many runners look for perfection. Even youngsters hesitate to undertake an activity if they do not feel they can do it well. The key here is to participate and not always be concerned with the outcome. This is especially important when beginning. Participate to get enjoyment from the activity as well as to achieve a certain level of fitness or running speed or distance.

9. Half a Workout Is Better Than None.   If it is impossible to have a full workout, a partial one is still of great benefit. Mental flexibility is as important as physical.

10. Give It Six to Eight Weeks.   Six to eight weeks is the amount of time it takes to develop a new habit. It is also how long it takes before you experience physiological changes in the body as a result of an exercise program. These are the long-lasting benefits that usually hook you on the activity and incline you toward greater participation.

11. Periodize Your Training.   To ensure constant improvement, you should periodize your training. This means the workouts change periodically so the type of training you have been doing will enable you to do the next, more intense, level of training. This cycle of periodic change (about four or more a year) prevents stagnation and boredom and enables you to reach your maximum potential.

12. Do Not Obsess Over Food.   Proper nutrition is critical to the best performances. However, being obsessive in relation to the foods and amounts eaten is detrimental to producing the best results. The key is to avoid thinking in terms of good foods or bad foods. Instead, think variety. All foods have value. The main items to beware of are saturated fats and trans-fatty acids, radiated foods, and processed foods.

13. Set Realistic Goals.   When goals are realistic they can be attained. You can then achieve the success and satisfaction needed to drive you on.

14. Give It Your Best Try.   Working out requires hard work, not only in the learning process but also in improving your ability. When you realize that it often takes hard work to receive any gains you desire, you will be more inclined to do the work to get the benefits. Tell yourself it will be worth it; remind yourself of the benefits.

15. Just Get Started.   Once you start in an effective manner, you will feel like continuing. Very often the most difficult part of an exercise or running program is taking the first step. Once it is taken, however, you overcome much of your anxiety and can really get into the activity.

16. Draw Up an Agreement.   Make an agreement with a coach, family member, or friend. Putting it in writing is a very important step for some individuals. With a specific contract, the actual days your workouts will take place and exactly what you will be doing is spelled out. The agreement should be long term and can include specific rewards and punishments.

17. Make It Enjoyable.   If you do not enjoy the activities in which you participate, you will quit. For example, running may not include all components of health-related physical fitness, but it is superior to starting and then quitting other activities that may include all the components. The key is to be active and do exercises that can help you regardless of whether they achieve all your goals at one time. This also applies to competitive running. The more you enjoy it, the more inclined you will be to put in the time and effort.

18. Say "Yes, I Can." Research shows that affirmations, simple positive statements that reflect your beliefs and intents, are powerful ways to keep on track or change for the better. When you think positively, you will get positive results. The goal is to focus on the process of making positive changes and on improvements, not on perfection. The great thing about running and running training is that they are not just ends in themselves. They are a means of helping achieve other things in life through a balanced, healthy lifestyle.

19. Keep an Eye on the Future. Focus more closely on where your running or fitness level will be in the next few months or even years. If you keep your goals in mind, especially long-term goals, you will be more likely to succeed and not be set back by any minor failures. This is a great way to maintain a positive, long-range outlook.

20. Visualize Success. Seeing yourself performing well in your imagination increases self-confidence. If you can see it and believe it, you can realize it.

In Conclusion

Although I can't present an exact workout for each of you, I have provided general guidelines on how the workouts should progress from the beginning of the year to the time of competition. You have a great arsenal of exercises from which to choose and different types of programs to bring about increases in strength, speed-strength, endurance, and speed. It is simply a matter of selecting the exercises and programs that will best enhance your abilities and incorporating them within the guidelines presented.

Many running programs do not follow these guidelines mainly because runners (especially sprinters) do not train on a year-round basis or do not stay in shape on a year-round basis. General conditioning and getting ready for running often take place in the pre-season. The early meets of the season are often used to prepare runners for more intense running. This is not the best way to become a better runner.

Some running programs even include heavy weight training at the beginning of the season. This interferes greatly with running technique, as does general conditioning work. All such work should be done well in advance of the competitive season. By adhering to the recommendations presented in this book you will be able to run your best and get better every year.

Appendix

The following services are available from Sports Training, Inc.:

- biomechanical analysis of your run
- analysis of your physical abilities
- a personalized exercise program
- technique enhancement

Contact us for more information about any of the equipment used in this book, or for information on filming your run or purchasing a record-keeping book with many workout tips, which can be used to evaluate your progress.

Sports Training, Inc.
P. O. Box 460429
Escondido, CA 92046
Telephone: (760) 480-0558
Fax: (760) 480-1277
Note: area code scheduled to change in winter 2000. New area code will be 442.
E-mail: sptstrng @ aol.com

Or visit our website at www.dryessis.com.

Index

About the Author

Michael Yessis, Ph.D., is president of Sports Training, Inc. and, during his forty years of working with athletes, has developed what has come to be known as the "Yessis System" for improving running speed. This three-step method has been used to coach athletes in football, soccer, baseball, and track so that they can improve their technique and speed.

Dr. Yessis serves on the advisory board and is the clinical advisor for the American Running Association. He has written more than 2,000 articles for many magazines and is a regular contributor for *Muscle and Fitness* magazine and *Peak Running Performance Newsletter.* He has also contributed to the magazine *Track and Field Coaches Review.*

He is the author ot ten books including *Kinesiology of Exercise* and *Explosive Golf* and has developed four videos.

Dr. Yessis currently resides in Escondido, CA with his family.